William Dello Russo

New York

TRAVEL **COOL**TURE | Be in the know

whitestar

Today's Paradigm

The news that the most densely populated city in the United States (with over eight and a half million inhabitants) is literally sinking beneath the weight of its over one million buildings has caused shock and some anxiety. Condemning it may be its own visionary urban form along with the rise in sea level.

Cities surrounded by water, such as Venice and Istanbul, have an allure, an oblivious attitude toward their own fragility. It's hard to find a description of Manhattan as evocative as Truman Capote's when he compares the island to a diamond iceberg floating in river water:

> **What makes it differ from one day to the next, as elusive and changeable as the clouds that quickly sweep over the Hudson, are the infinite stories that unfold beneath the skyscrapers between their lit and unlit windows, amid noisy and chaotic traffic intersections.**

◂ The Vessel at Hudson Yards

New York is the capital of the twentieth century, with all its delusions, conflicts, and shattered dreams, a dream city for those who have visited it but once, and those who have never seen it and never will, save in the movies or in a coffee-table book.

The two words of its name generate fantasies, visions, mirages. It's the epitome of ambition, the incarnation of desire, the promise of an ever-new world. Admired, envied, or detested, New York is the paradigm of the present, a leader that has only been rivaled a few times in history.

Even after the 2001 attempt to break its hold, its pieces were collected, dusted off, and painfully reassembled. A pulsating city whose multi-ethnic neighborhoods spill over into glittering financial enclaves and whose brick buildings are mirrored in towers that defy fear, disorder, and ugliness and overturn all aesthetic conventions. A city of nostalgia, in which everyone left something of their land of origin, even generations ago. A city with a green core, a memory of an island transformed into a concrete jungle. A city of paper and celluloid, retold and filmed by anyone wielding a pen or operating a camera. A fierce but also miraculous city, where one can be anyone or risk becoming no one after losing everything, where one can hide and expose oneself to others and oneself. A global city, where beauty and tragedy manage to coexist and astonish, and that has managed to keep clinging to its indomitable spirit.

→ Little Island, a floating island

Far from being a conventional guide, this volume reveals what actually makes New York a unique place.

Anyone who loves traveling will be eager to learn about the culture of specific places and the legends that have contributed to their fame—such as those recounted in the following chapters.

Melting Pot

"New York is a different country. Maybe it ought to have a separate government. Everybody thinks differently, acts differently. They just don't know what the hell the rest of the United States is."

– Henry Ford

← The Statue of Liberty in New York Harbor, with Ellis Island in the background

All one needs to do is take one step into the city—or even the airport—to realize the incredible ethnic melting pot in which New York simmers. Today, approximately one in four Americans has an ancestor who passed through Ellis Island, once the main gateway to the American Dream. For Barack Obama, no one in America can truly claim to be indigenous. A vibrant and creative mix that makes the Babel of the East Coast unique in the world, but that in the past—and even now—has not made it impervious to stereotypes, segregation, and ethnic tensions. The conflict between those who oppose and favor immigration has never ultimately been resolved.

New York City is by far the largest city in the United States in terms of population, and one of the few in which each of four racial groups—white, Latino, African American, and Asian, in order of magnitude—in addition to being concentrated in certain neighborhoods, accounts for over ten percent of the total population. This amounts to 8,335,897 inhabitants (data as of 1 July 2022), a noticeable drop of nearly half a million inhabitants since the pre-pandemic period, save in Manhattan, where the demographic growth refuses to slow down. Nonetheless, due to overcrowding, the "sanctuary city" currently finds itself lacking beds and services for immigrants.

The mother of all who are exiled

The Statue of Liberty was inaugurated at the entrance to New York Harbor at the mouth of the Hudson River on October 28, 1886. Most surprising are the dimensions of the sculpture (forty-six meters high), especially when the nose and index fingers of the copper lady are compared—one being 4.9 feet, the others each 8—to those of a human being. These details don't have to be technically refined, simply visible from a distance. More than creating a beautiful work of art, the sculptor Bartholdi and the engineer Eiffel demonstrated to the world the astonishing marvels of the Iron Age. Three months later, the grand endeavor of the Eiffel Tower got its start in Paris. A gift from France on the occasion of the first centenary of the American Revolution, the monument commemorating the independence of the United States of America ended up embodying the "freedom that illuminates the world" from the moment it was unveiled.

In that same year, almost three hundred and thirty thousand immigrants landed in the United States. The descriptions, first- and second-hand, of the sight of that sculpture with its right hand holding the torch to the sky and its left arm supporting a slab inscribed with the date of the Declaration of Independence, always betray some tremulousness.

Those immigrants sailing in third class may only have seen a stylized Statue of Liberty printed on a brochure distributed by the thousands of agencies or shipping companies that offered, along with a journey on a steamship, the prospect of a completely new life. The reports recall a kaleidoscope of emotions—tears, laughter, dancing, prayers—exploding at the sight of that beacon of salvation immersed in fog or illuminated by the sun. In 1935, the Polish author and future Nobel Prize laureate Isaac Bashevis Singer landed in America as well, though he already knew all about the statue: "My mother used to read the Yiddish letters that emigrants sent their parents, and they were always writing about the statue. They said that when they finally saw the statue, their hearts calmed down: 'I know nothing bad can happen to me.' They believed in her as if she were some sort of goddess."

In 1903, a plaque inscribed with a sonnet by the poet Emma Lazarus was mounted on the statue's pedestal. Its middle lines read: "Give me your tired, your poor, your huddled masses yearning to breathe free." At the threshold of the twentieth century and the height of the great transatlantic migrations, millions of men, women, and children had already passed beneath the shadow of Lady Liberty, eager to escape their own lands and their unchanging conditions, though their future, waiting to be written, would often prove as merciless as the one they had left behind.

America's golden door

In the year 1907, nearly 1.3 million arrivals were registered at Ellis Island, a figure never attained again. The numbers offer a somewhat impersonal

↑ A family of immigrants on the dock at Ellis Island (1925)

account of the phenomenon of migration to the New World, but are no less impressive for all that. The wave of migration to the United States between 1840 and 1914 is said to be the largest in modern history. Until around the mid-nineteenth century, the East Coast welcomed people flocking primarily from northern and central Europe, from England, Ireland, Germany. The second phase saw the arrival of southern and eastern Europeans, from Italy, the Balkans, Russia. Clinging to their miserable bundles, they fled from poverty, from unstable or cruel political regimes, from religious persecution, from natural disasters. There were the Irish starved by the Great Famine; the Italians, mainly from the south, crushed by the decline following the unification, by the poverty of their countryside, by the consequences of the Messina earthquake; the Jews escaping the Russian pogroms. The bottom of the melting pot was in the process of being cast.

The ocean liners departed from the great European ports—Liverpool, Rotterdam, Le Havre, Genoa, Naples—loaded with human lives and hopes.

→ Checking for infectious diseases on Ellis Island

Some cast balls of wool to relatives remaining on the pier while holding on to a strand of yarn that trembled in mid-air before slipping out of their hands. A journey full of dangers, the first—and often last—ever taken by the vast majority of passengers, and one during which lives were destroyed not only by storms at sea, but also by malnutrition, cholera, and violence on board: it's been estimated that among those in steerage, one in seven migrants didn't make it alive; percentage-wise, the number was far higher for children.

Island of tears, island of hope

Approximately twelve million people passed through **Ellis Island** from 1892, the year in which the world's most imposing migrant control center

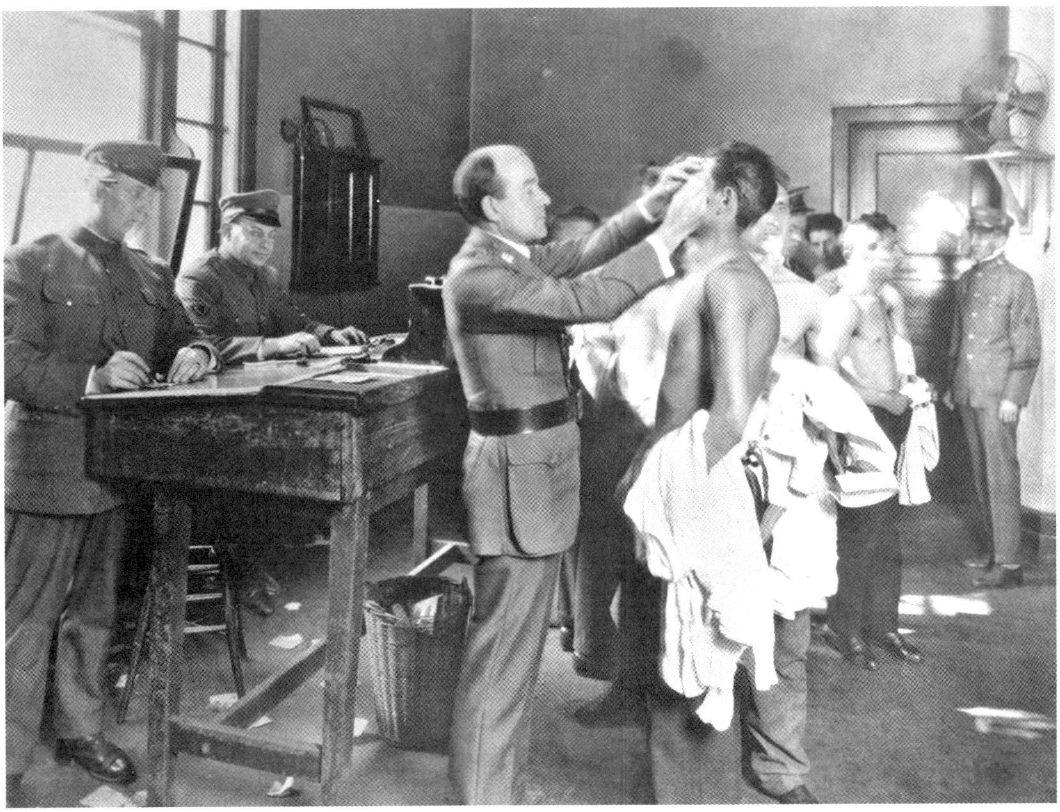

opened its doors, to 1924, when the Immigration Act placed strict limits on the quota of newcomers. The "golden portal" closed for good due, in 1954, to an unprecedented organizational apparatus. The establishment of a federal "hub" at the entrance to the port of New York was essential for dealing with the phenomenon in the late 19th century. The other, western, gate, lay in San Francisco.

Films, novels, and accounts always describe the voyage, the arrival, and the verification process in a vivid and touching manner. Medical checkups caused the most anxiety—not so much the general ones that took place on board (first- and second-class passengers, after disembarking in Manhattan or Brooklyn, were free to leave), but the decisive "six-second" inspection at Ellis Island. That was the amount of time doctors dedicated to each immigrant. Afterwards they might come out marked in chalk with a circled X (indicating mental illness), with an L (a disability), or with the letters CT,

standing for trachoma, a dangerous eye disease sometimes checked by the doctors with a not necessarily sanitary iron hook.

The interrogation regarding the reasons for expatriation, financial means, criminal record, and commitment to reuniting with some family member in the country was no less stressful. In practice, immigrants had to demonstrate that they could take care of themselves, that they would not burden the rest of the country, and that they posed no threat.

Despite the anticipatory dread of this eight-hour process, only two percent of migrants were sent back home. Nonetheless, fear penetrated deep into the dark, dirty, and overcrowded underbelly of the ship for many reasons: unfamiliarity with the language (only one out of two emigrants had any knowledge of English); dealing with authorities capable of shattering the hopes of a lifetime in an instant; temporary separation of families during the interrogation process; the detention of some family members for further questioning; and the fear of having embarked on a futile journey. It is no coincidence that Ellis Island earned the hardly endearing nickname of "Island of Tears."

Old and new migrations

According to estimates, eighty percent of immigrants got through the checkpoint (capitalism had an ever-greater need for unskilled labor). One in five emigrants—those with tuberculosis, suspicious political ties, waiting to join someone, etc.—were detained on the island and, after days or weeks, released or, in the worst case, sent back to the Old World. Only a few considered relocating to other large cities in the eastern United States. Most remained in New York, which was prospering, enriching itself, and rising. The government was forced to issue a series of acts that barred entry to those deemed pernicious to social cohesion (e.g., the illiterate, anarchists, prostitutes), and went so far as to target specific groups (primarily the Chinese).

◂ Registration hall at Ellis Island (1912)

↑ Baggage left behind by immigrants at Ellis Island

To visit Ellis Island today is to pay tribute to the stories of these immigrants. The excitement, the odors, and the various languages that flooded the Great Hall have given way to a well-organized and highly educational Immigration Museum, where people can search for the names of their ancestors and listen to oral accounts. The National Park Service's Ellis Island Oral History Project preserves interviews and testimony of approximately two thousand immigrants (https://heritage.statueofliberty.org/oral-history-library). It is impossible to absorb millions of stories, but the underlying coordinates are the same: the difficulties of a potentially fatal voyage, the experience at Ellis Island, the language barrier. And, afterwards, the struggle to preserve one's cultural identity and traditions while adapting to new ones.

"To me, Ellis Island is the ultimate place of exile, that is, the place where the place is absent, the non-place, the nowhere." The verses of

→ The main building on Ellis Island, today a museum dedicated to immigration

French writer Georges Perec go straight to the heart of the matter, which is about "wandering, dispersion, diaspora." Ellis Island remains an obligatory stop in our era, in which migration is likewise a distinctive feature. Many emigrants returned to their homeland after having put aside a nest egg ("birds of passage," as they were called), but many stayed put. By now, the millions of foreigners who passed through the island as well as their descendants can say that they are fully American, even if the pot has not melted all ties to Europe. Today, many wonder whether the same can be said of the new generations of immigrants. Integration is an ever-evolving process, driven by the determination of the generations who have called and continue to call this city "home." And the Statue of Liberty, forever present in the urban landscape, continues to serve as a gigantic visual reminder.

Vertical Symphony

"Unlike Rome, New York has never learned the art of growing old by playing on all its pasts. Its present invents itself, from hour to hour, in the act of throwing away its previous accomplishments and challenging the future."

– Michel de Certeau, 1980

◂ The Empire State Building towering over a spectacular view of Midtown

The Council on Tall Buildings and Urban Habitat (Ctbuh), a Chicago-based international organization that focuses on tall buildings and sustainable urban design, ranks New York City third in the world when it comes to the number of buildings that exceed 150 meters (492 feet) in height (it has three hundred and fourteen) and fourth in terms of buildings over 200 meters tall (656 feet) (it has ninety-five). If we're speaking of buildings over 300 meters (984 feet) tall, it ranks second; of these it has at least sixteen. Although today the city has to reckon with Dubai, Shenzen, and Hong Kong, the period that has witnessed history's most daring architecture does not yet seem to be over.

According to Ctbuh (ctbuh.org), New York, with its more than six thousand skyscrapers, is the tallest city in the United States and all of North America. It is home to the Freedom Tower, which, at over five hundred and forty-one meters (1774 feet), is the sixth-tallest building on the planet (topping the list is Dunai's Burj Khalifa, one and a half times as tall). However, the city's most significant record must be sought elsewhere: namely, in the fact that its endless and constantly changing skyline of towers and bridges is the most iconic one in the world—an eclectic array of styles amid valleys of glass, steel, and concrete—the fruit of ingenuity, derring-do, unbridled megalomania, and the open violation of the law of gravity, but invariably triumphant over their naysayers.

Reaching up to God

The shock of 9/11 passed fairly quickly in the field of architecture. The rate of growth since then has reached a feverish pitch, both in terms of the number of skyscrapers built and their height. By now, around twenty supertall structures have been completed or are in the process of being so. It is obviously no coincidence that the Freedom Tower, the supreme symbol of rebirth, is the tallest structure in the United States (see page 94). From the elegant and deliberately "transparent" **New York Times Building** (2007) by Renzo Piano to Skidmore, Owings & Merrill's **175 Park Avenue**, which will top at nearly five hundred meters (1640 feet), which is expected to be completed by 2030, the main requisites are resistance, safety, high-tech features, and sustainability. Between these lies a panoply of architectural languages, the result of our fragmented times. There is the deconstructivist **Bank of America tower** and the less pronounced one at **One Vanderbilt**.

→ 432 Park Avenue, with the Sony (formerly AT&T) Building in the foreground

There is **Central Park Tower**, whose reflections recall the play of clouds and sky in Magritte's paintings, and the gigantic tetris from which the **Spiral** seems to be made.

Then there's the spindly **432 Park Avenue**, more like a column than a building (a "horrible waffle," according to its critics), and the equally

slender **111 West 57th Street** (or Steinway Tower), the slimmest skyscraper in the world, whose grainy profile casts a long shadow over Central Park. Skinny and super rich—as Edwin Heathcote points out in the *Financial Times*—these, like the millionaires for whom they have been designed, represent an epochal reversal of the aggregation principle that distinguished the early skyscrapers of the 1920s and 1930s; today 99.99% of the world's population is denied access to the ultra-luxury lobbies of Billionaires' Row.

The first steps up toward the sky

As a building typology, the skyscraper did not originate in New York. It was the great concentration of capital and the practical need to create office space for the many white-collar workers displaced by the Big Fire of 1871 that razed Chicago to the ground that led to the birth of the vertical metropolis. As decisive as these historical-economic factors, were the technical innovations. These included a super-robust load-bearing structure of steel pillars and beams on which wall panels and large windows could be mounted; the invention of the electric elevator, which eliminated the need to climb stairs on foot and inverted the commercial value of the street level and the upper floors for good; air conditioning; and artificial illumination.

However, it was in Manhattan rather than Chicago that both the unchecked population growth caused by immigration, and the dreams, ambitions, and neuroses of rampant capitalism found their physical form in ever-more-vertiginous towers that stood in open competition with each other, reviving, so it seemed, the rivalry among Europe's medieval cathedrals (albeit with a diametrically opposed purpose). And while the marshland of Chicago forced a limit of 260 feet (79 meters) on the height of buildings, the stony island between the Hudson and the East River has seen its artificial horizon rise to infinity. As for form, New York's skyscrapers recall Mesopotamian ziggurats (or wedding cakes) due to a law imposing setbacks that was passed as early as 1916 in order to mitigate shadows that cast streets and other buildings in darkness even at midday.

The weight of history

At the unveiling of the Flatiron Building, the *New York Tribune* noted that the "crowds were looking at the building with their heads so thrown back that their necks seemed ready to snap." There were no instant accolades for what has now become one of the indisputable icons of Manhattan; more often than not, it was berated for its retro style, the oddity of its wedge shape ("a stingy piece of cake," "a rabbit warren"), or cynical jokes about its stability due to the gusts of wind channeled by the building. Completed in 1902, the "steamship prow" or "flatiron" is among the oldest steel-framed skyscrapers to have survived. Planning something along the lines of a grand Renaissance palazzo, architect Daniel H. Burnham seems not to have wished to break ties with the Old Continent. Squeezed between Broadway and Fifth Avenue on a difficult lot the shape of an isosceles triangle, the Flatiron, when viewed from head on, evokes a gigantic Greek column complete with base, shaft, and capital. Visible from the side view is its classical tripartite division, accentuated by protruding cornices: the stone base, twenty-two floors decorated with terra-cotta reliefs in the Beaux Arts style, and, finally, an attic.

The Flatiron was never the tallest building in the world, but the Woolworth Building (241 meters/790 feet) held that honor for seventeen years, inaugurating the upward-headed trend pursued by future skyscrapers. Nearly three times the height of the Flatiron, this lay "bell tower" was completed in 1913 with ribs, ornaments, and pinnacles inspired by European Gothic and neo-Gothic towers. On a bracket inside, architect Cass Gilbert had himself sculpted as a medieval saint holding a model of the building in his hands.

The three Giants

Paradoxically, the fiercest and most exciting battle for the sky, conducted in secret or with trickery, took place in the years of the Great Depression, just as Fritz Lang was anticipating everything in his visionary *Metropolis* (1927). The race for height saw fierce rivalry between the Woolworth Building and the **Bank of Manhattan Trust Building** on Wall Street until November 1929 (the precise date remains highly controversial), when the spire of the **Chrysler Building** was unveiled to Americans and broke the Eiffel Tower's record as the tallest structure in the world. William Van Alen, the architect, created a spectacular crown in a chrome-nickel-steel alloy that culminated in a gigantic needle, with motifs recalling car radiators and wheels in an infinite race toward progress. The spire appeared miraculously after the rest of the structure had been finished: to overcome Chrysler's rival, the Bank of Manhattan, the top was manufactured clandestinely in workshops inside the building and hoisted into the air in a mere hour and a half. The building's shininess, its metal gargoyles, and the photographs of Margaret Bourke-White, a pioneering photojournalist, transform it into an exemplar of Art Deco and make us instantly forget earlier critiques that declared it an "upside-down swordfish" or "oversized jukebox."

Barely a year later, the scepter passed to the **Empire State Building**, which held on to it for nearly forty years, or until the construction of the Twin Towers. Legend has it that business magnate John J. Raskob raised a pencil in the air and simply asked architect William F. Lamb: "How high can you make it so it doesn't fall over?" The rest of the story is better known: the Great Depression, the difficulty of renting out the building's empty spaces, and the malicious nickname "Empty State Building," the post-war recovery, and the continuing success of the structure's observatory with its superb views of four states—without forgetting Lewis Hine's still quite powerful photos of workers suspended hundreds of feet above the ground with no protective gear and the heartbreaking finale of the 1933 movie *King Kong*.

↑ The supremely elegant silhouette of the Chrysler Building

The crisis into which the world sank in 1929 did not even graze John D. Rockefeller Jr., the financier and heir to the richest man in history. Today, **Rockefeller Center's** immense Art Deco media center, a veritable "Babylonian dream," brings to mind a magical ice-skating rink,

↑ One of the entrances into Rockefeller Center

To read

- Ayn Rand, ***The Fountainhead*** (1946)
- Karl Sabbagh, ***Skyscraper*** (1989)
- Sarah Bradford Landau and Carl W. Condit, ***Rise of the New York Skyscraper*** (1996)
- Lewis Mumford, ***Passeggiando per New York*** (2000)
- Antonino Terranova, ***Grattacieli*** (2003)
- Bruce Marshall, ***Building New York*** (2005)
- Alice Sparberg Alexiou, ***The Flatiron*** (2010)
- ***Architects Institute of America, AIA Guide to New York City*** (2020)
- Dirk Stichweh, ***NY Skyscrapers*** (2016)

the most photographed Christmas tree in the world, an institution like Radio City Music Hall, and the world's first underground garage. Back then it reconfigured an entire chunk of Midtown. Several figures are enough to provide an idea of the "largest construction project since the pyramids": to bring it into existence, two hundred and twenty-eight buildings were razed to the ground, nearly four thousand tenants were displaced, and between forty and sixty thousand people were employed—or sixty percent of the available workforce at the time.

↳Manhattan's most refined skyscraper, the Seagram Building, is a masterpiece by Ludwig Mies van der Rohe and Philip Johnson. Completed in 1958, this crystal box is special in that its front is set back from Park Avenue: a touch of genius by the Bauhaus master, who, instead of keeping it hidden, set off its presence with a plaza that allows it to be grasped with a single look.

Modern, postmodern

Once the financial momentum resumed in the 1950s, the International Style took over, enriching the panorama with creations quite different from those of the Deco giants of the 1930s. These are either loved or hated: the United Nations headquarters based on a plan by Le Corbusier, the crystalline **Lever House** by Skidmore, Owings & Merrill, and the **Seagram Building** by Ludwig Mies van der Rohe and Philip Johnson. But there's also the monolithic octagon of the **Pan Am Building** (now MetLife), which a 1987 survey revealed as the building that the city's residents most dreamed of demolishing (also because it sits right on top of Grand Central Station), and the late and flashy Trump Tower, a triumph of unchecked free-market capitalism complete with indoor waterfall.

Postmodernism experimented with new kinds of roofs—such as the one inclined at forty-five degrees at **Citicorp Center**, a building raised above the ground so that the space below it can be put to use—as well as new forms that broke the monotony of the parallelepiped—such as the giant lipstick compact evoked by **885 Third Avenue** designed by Philip Johnson, who, in his **AT&T** (today **Sony**) **Building** proposed an anachronistic return to pink granite and the use of the pediment.

We deliberately leave Minoru Yamasaki's vanished **Twin Towers** to the end: an entity so out of scale, unusual in its duality, and harboring such powerful symbolism that even today many find it difficult to process the revised skyline.

↳ The skyline along the Hudson has changed quite abruptly in the last decade and will change again. The oversized skyscrapers of Hudson Yards don't seem to engage in any kind of dialogue with each other, but their impact is impressive and has affected the image of these new Roaring Twenties.

MoMA
Alexande
Calder

The Empire of Art

"In the past, dominant nations had always plundered works of art from their predecessors; [. . .] America was taking a leading place among nations and had, therefore, the right to obtain art wherever she could."

– Stanford White

Thus did the American neoclassical architect sum up the attitude of the Second Industrial Revolution and the American Renaissance toward art. Today a nation born a mere two and a half centuries ago possesses a cultural arsenal that causes ever more envy on the opposite shores of the Atlantic. Disentangling the cultural threads tying Europe to the East Coast is a fascinating endeavor, one in which the main roles are played by collectors, philanthropists, patrons, and a torrent of dollars. New York alone is home to countless museums that grew from individual private collections. To realize the full scale of this phenomenon, all one needs to do is to stop and check the legenda beneath the pieces in the museums or check out the names of the galleries in which they are on display.

← MoMA's unmistakable logo

In Europe, museums arose over the course of the last three centuries, originating in the increasingly stratified collections of princes, sovereigns, and powerful families, or else the rich legacy of the Church. In the United States, by contrast, collecting was a phenomenon relegated to individuals, linked to their inexhaustible capital, yet destined to become public property.

The first private art gallery in the U.S. was founded in New York in 1832 by Luman Reed, a retired wholesale merchant. Between the last two decades of that century and World War I, a flood of artworks poured into the country in a genuine exodus from Europe and the Near East. Thanks to their preferences and choices, railroad, mining, finance, and commerce magnates, craving cultural legitimacy, helped forge the taste of the entire nation and pull it away from hackneyed genre painting to the pinnacles of modern art within a very short time.

Today, American museums continue to acquire masterpieces and fund research at breakneck speed thanks to private donations and the generous contributions of philanthropists and volunteers. New York City has a hundred museums that cover all kinds of fields, from art to mathematics, archeology to jazz, science to cinema. Below we cover three of them, recounting their particular "biographies."

The art mogul

The second wife of **John Pierpont Morgan's** (1837-1913) once said that her husband would buy anything from a pyramid to the tooth of Mary Magdalene. There's an object in the **Metropolitan Museum of Art** whose preciousness and contents are atten-

tion-grabbing. It consists of a 14th-15th-century Tuscan reliquary that holds—according to tradition—that very tooth of the Magdalene. It took Morgan only twenty years to amass a collection that was valued

▲ The Metropolitan Museum of Art

↳ In an extraordinary leap across space and time, centuries of the European Middle Ages merge together at The Cloisters, the branch of the Met in Inwood devoted to this historical era. Here one can admire panel paintings and tapestries, illuminated manuscripts, stained-glass windows, and ivory carvings. Most striking, however, are the entire monumental complexes taken from small villages in the Pyrenees (such as the cloister from the Benedictine monastery of Saint-Michel-de-Cuxa) or French abbeys, and reassembled stone by stone across the ocean.

at no less than 60 million dollars at the time. A steel tycoon, banker, and financier who twice saved the United States from a financial crash, Morgan was an Italian Renaissance prince, pope, or a French king reincarnated, an enlightened philanthropist and oligarch equally eager for power and splendor. He snatched up entire art collections in Europe and Egypt with the same voracity with which he bought railway lines and organized industrial trusts. **"No price is too great for a work of unquestioned beauty and known authenticity,"** he declared. His goals were to amass the largest art collection in America and thus make travel to the Old World unnecessary, and to enrich the museum that he himself had helped establish and of which he became director.

Upon Morgan's death in 1914, his entire collection—probably the richest ever compiled by a private individual—was put on display. This was the first and last time it could be admired in its entirety.

The Chinese porcelain, Fragonard paintings, Renaissance bronzes, and Limoges enamels were later dispersed. About half the objects were donated to the Metropolitan Museum, most notably Egyptian and Hellenic antiquities, Byzantine enamels and ivories, gems, Gothic ivories, a large altarpiece by Raphael, and Assyrian reliefs from the palace of Ashurnasirpal II. Today, the spirit of Morgan—as well as those of the Rothschilds, Vanderbilts, Robert Lehman, the Rockefellers, and the Havemeyers—lingers in the fabulous galleries of the Met, one of the richest and most comprehensive collections in the world. With its 1.5 million objects from every corner of the Earth, it has truly come to deserve the title of the "museum of all museums."

Intrepid women

A mutual friendship with the painter Arthur B. Davies, a chance encounter in Egypt, a lunch with high-society friends, and the bitter admission that the museum network in the U.S. was deficient when it came to modern European art. The spark that led to the foundation of the **MoMA**, the museum that still dictates taste in modern art, ignited the drive of the three women who took up the challenge facing much of New York's cultural elite: **Lillie Plummer Bliss (1864-1931)**, whose early passion for modern art, despite her mother's disapproval, led to her purchase of paintings by Cézanne, Renoir, and Degas; art instructor **Mary Quinn Sullivan (1877-1939)**, whose predilection for Modigliani, Matisse, and Toulouse-Lautrec dated to the late 1920s, and **Abby Aldrich Rockefeller (1874-1948)**, whose contacts, enthusiasm, and finances were what really made it happen. Profoundly moved by Vincent van Gogh's miserable end, and despite her husband's—the entrepreneur John D. Rockefeller Jr.—aversion to modern art, she envisioned a museum that would help emerging American artists and educate the public.

The first exhibition held at the museum, founded a few days after the Wall Street crash, took place in six rooms on the twelfth floor of a Fifth Avenue building and honored four post-Impressionist painters: Cézanne, Gauguin, Seurat, and Van Gogh. Forty-seven thousand tickets were sold, and a legend was born. The museum's mission was to have a collection as "permanent as those of a river whose waters are in constant flux." It was only in 1939 that MoMA found its definitive home in a marble, glass, and steel building on land owned by the Rockefellers.

If Morgan never purchased a modern work, Alfred H. Barr, the director of the museum from its inception until 1943, and afterwards the Director of Collections from 1947 to 1967, drafted the 1929 plan as follows: "In time the Museum would probably expand beyond the narrow limits of painting and sculpture in order to include departments devoted to drawings, prints, and photography, typography, the arts of design in commerce and industry, architecture (a collection of projects, and maquettes), stage designing, furniture, and the decorative arts. Not the least important collection might be the filmotek, a library of films."

→ Inside MoMA

Upon his death, he could never have imagined that in 2010 MoMA's collections would include emoji and Artificial Intelligence, that it would be here that Marina Abramović would stage one of her most powerful performances (*The Artist Is Present*, 2010), and that the museum would be expanded by Diller Scofidio + Renfro (2019), in one of the many forms—but certainly not the final one—in its history.

Aristocracy and the industrial

"I want a temple of spirit, a monument!" the Baroness **Hilla von Rebay** (1890-1967) declared to Frank Lloyd Wright. She had never seen a building designed by this master of organic architecture, whereas he was under the impression that the letter he had received had been written by a man. But it was actually the mind and taste of a woman that lay behind the **Solomon R. Guggenheim Museum**, a structure that has revolutionized museum architecture for good. Inside, visitors are invited to walk down a unique, wrap-around spiral along which works are put on display. It was the Prussian Baroness who got in touch with Wright. Having grown up in one of the most artistically creative periods in European history amid movements such as Dadaism, abstractionism, and expressionism, Hilla used art and spirituality as a guide through life. Her search led her to "non-objective" art: that is, one with no recognizable subject.

It was in the *Empire City*, where she landed in 1927, that the enterprise got its start with her meeting with Irene Rothschild and her husband, the incredibly wealthy mining industrialist Solomon R. Guggenheim, several consultations, and then purchases of works by artists such as Wassily Kandinsky, Rudolf Bauer, and others in Europe on behalf of the tycoon. Abstract and non-objective art wrought profound changes in the nature of the couple's original collection. Starting with an apartment in the Plaza Hotel, von Rebay moved the collection to ever larger spaces and became the first director of the Museum of Non-Objective Painting, the precursor of today's Guggenheim.

→ The Solomon R. Guggenheim Museum

Accusations of espionage by both the Gestapo and the FBI, her early contact with Wright, whom she had approached to design the building for displaying the collection, the tycoon's death in 1949 and the end of his protection, along with a fatal mix of personal ambition and rivalry, all combined to eventually force the baroness to resign from her post as director of the museum and put up with the ultimate insult of not even receiving an invitation to the Fifth Avenue building's inauguration on October 21, 1959. Unlike the tycoon and the architect, who, respectively, died ten years and six months before the museum's completion, she at least was lucky enough to be able to admire it. Despite the heavy criticism of the museum, whose form was compared to that of a toilet or a washing machine, Wright kept his promise to his client to make the Metropolitan Museum "look like a Protestant barn."

Nicknames, Symbols, and Branding

"New York, New York—so nice, they had to name it twice"

– from George Russell's song Manhattan *sung by Jon Hendricks*

Big Apple, Big City, Big Burg, Fun City, Fifty-First State, Gotham City, Metropolis, or simply the City to underscore its uniqueness . . . New York's hundred nicknames speak to the countless identities embedded in its multifaceted genetic code and reflected in its flag, the emblem of the city. Nonetheless, the logo of the iconic metropolitan brand —the most effective ever produced— dates to the 1960s.

← "The city that never sleeps" is one of New York's most appropriate epithets

The etymologist Barry Popik *(barrypopik.com)* has counted a hundred nicknames for the city, a record that testifies to its fame and allure. Although many of these, as one might expect, were short-lived and incapable of outlasting the fashion and times that generated them, the most famous of all, the Big Apple, has old and mysterious origins with a murky history.

Nickname

Working with Professor Gerald Cohen, Popik dug up the roots of the metropolis's successful epithet par excellence. It's known for certain that in 1924, John J. Fitz Gerald, the sports columnist of the *New York Morning Telegraph*, initiated a new column called "Around the Big Apple." The expression derived from the slang used by African American grooms working at the New Orleans racetrack to refer to "the big break," the kind that brings in lots of money. "The Big Apple. The dream of every lad that ever threw a leg over a thoroughbred and the goal of all horsemen," Fitz Gerald clarified in his column. "There's only one Big Apple. That's New York."

However, it was back in 1909 that, in his book *The Wayfarer in New York*, Edward S. Martin compared the states metaphorically to an apple tree, whose roots dig deep into the Mississippi Valley and whose branches stretch from one ocean to another, and whose largest fruit is New York City. But this tree, Martin went on, did not really like this fruit, which sucked up more sap than the others did. . . . In contrast to **Big Burg** and many others, this epithet has enjoyed lasting success and even today evokes a beautiful, juicy, luscious apple with all its possibilities that can nonetheless sometimes be tainted with vice and debauchery. Paying tribute to the city, the Mets have turned the apple into a fun pop icon.

→ Big Apple Corner at 54th Street and Broadway

Although certain sobriquets—such as "Frog and Toe" or "Babylonian Bedlam"—remain pretty obscure, **"the city that never sleeps"** is one that's instantly comprehensible. Used on occasion to describe some of the city's livelier neighborhoods, it was enshrined only in 1979 by Frank Sinatra on a record cover of a song first performed by Liza Minnelli in the musical *New York, New York* two years prior: "I want to wake up in a city that never sleeps," followed by "And find I'm a number one, top of the list / King of the hill."

It was the English, who replaced the Dutch in 1664, who granted the city its official name. For the Dutch West India Company, the mouth of the Hudson River had served as an ideal site for a fort from which

to conduct their fur-trade emporium. The colony of New Amsterdam (actually, Nieuw Amsterdam) was founded ca. 1625 on the southernmost tip of the island of Manhattan. The first thing the British did was to rename the settlement after the Duke of York, brother of Charles II and the future King James II. For a few months between 1673 and the following year, the Dutch reconquered Manhattan and named the city **Nieuw Orange**, in tribute to the royal dynasty of that name. What's interesting is how a city that never served as the capital either of a state or a kingdom received the prestigious epithet of **"Empire City."** To trace the origin of this term, we must presumably go back to 1785, when George Washington showed his appreciation for New Yorkers' commitment during the American Revolution. It was on that occasion that he designated it for the first time—and unexpectedly—as "the Seat of the Empire."

Flags and seals

As a symbol of U.S. identity, the flag has no rivals. This was evident after the 9/11 attacks, when, while the rubble was still smoldering, every state was bedecked with the patriotic Stars and Stripes. An infinite number of various flags can be seen fluttering in New York: the Stars and Stripes, flags of the city and its five boroughs (Manhattan's is nearly identical to NYC's), and those of the state. The last of these is easily recognizable because standing against its blue background are two personifications, Liberty and Justice, between which a coat of arms surmounted by an eagle bears the word "Excelsior."

The flag of the city relates a great deal about the city's unique history and character, with an unexpected twist. A mix of stories about the past, it has often been criticized for its old-fashioned style, one too bound up with the Old World. Approved only in 1915, it remains European in its use of the tricolor (severing all historical and, particularly, cultural ties is im-

→ The flag of New York City

possible), in this case, blue, white, and orange, which refer to the Dutch flag. Standing out in the center against a white field is the blue seal of the city, whose components are worth describing with care: the bald eagle is the symbol of the United States as a whole; the Native American evokes the indigenous cultures that pre-existed the Europeans' arrival; the sailor holding a plumb bob in his hand represents the colonizers in this corner of the world. The blades of the windmill in the coat of arms are a precise reference to the Netherlands, as well as to the economic importance of the milling of grain and the country's monopoly over that trade—an idea reinforced by the two barrels of flour placed on either side. The two rodents too evoke the European country, in particular its fruitful trade in the furs and skins of beavers, otters, and other animals, luxury products in high demand in the fashion and clothing industry of the Old World. Finally, the cryptic inscription on the outer frame, "Sigillum Civitatis Novi Eboraci," underscores the city's relationship with the United Kingdom, the brooding father from whom it would later distance itself: Eburacum or Eboracum is the Latin name of the modern city of York.

The most intriguing aspect of New York's flag lies in something else, however. For six decades, until 1974, the date on the seal was 1664, the year in which Peter Stuyvesant, the last Dutch governor, ceded the colony to the British. Most historians, however, agree that 1625, the year inserted after the flag's restyling, is arbitrary, since the first settlers landed on Governors Island one or possibly two years earlier. These had been Belgian Walloons who had sought asylum in the Netherlands in order to escape religious persecution by the Spanish Inquisition.

Manhattan (allegedly derived from a term meaning "the place where wood is gathered to make bows" in Munsee dialect), a cattle range and rich hunting ground for the natives, was "purchased" by the Dutch only in 1626 in one of the most sensational "real estate transactions" in history, the result of a misunderstanding and the differing concepts of private property on the part of the Lenape, who did not personally own the land, and the Europeans, who, by contrast, were eager to obtain it. The Dutch didn't grant the settlement an official city charter until 1653. Perhaps turning back the hands of the historical clock was a way of diminishing the British contribution to the establishment of New York and outdoing Boston, which boasts of its foundation in 1630.

I ♥ NY

No other city in the world can boast a more recognizable, effective, and long-lasting visual brand. This it owes to **Milton Glaser**, who adored Piero della Francesca and studied in Bologna with the painter Giorgio Morandi. The precision, clarity, and formal tension of the two Italian masters seem to reverberate in the creations of the Bronx-born, humanist-oriented designer, who passed away in 2020 at age 91. Although his fame is always associated with this logo, Glaser was already a mature and recognized artist at the time of the commission: it was he who came up with the famous psychedelic poster adorning the cover of the album of Bob Dylan's *Greatest Hits* (1966), which shows the artist in profile with his hair in multicolored coiled strands, and who founded *New York Magazine*, one of the most successful periodicals of all time.

By the mid-1970s, New York was on the verge of economic collapse and had plunged into a downward spiral of day-to-day anxiety and violence. It was the Department of Commerce that asked the Wells Rich Greene advertising agency to come up with a promotional campaign to bring back tourists and combat the city's bad reputation. Legend has it that Glaser, commissioned by the agency, scrawled the logo in red crayon on an envelope while riding in a taxi (today the sketch is at MoMA). The artist himself noted that his subliminal inspiration may have come from another famous American work, Robert Indiana's LOVE, in which the "L" and the "O" are superimposed over the "V" and "E." He achieved this objective in a "simple" rebus consisting of only four elements: a word (I) plus a two-letter acronym (NY) bound together by a simple red heart, a forerunner of the emoticon. In 1977, reading the pictogram of a heart as the verb "love" was by no means a logical process. Written in the easily legible American Typewriter font, the entire composition is imbued with an unconditional declaration of love for the city, similar—as Glaser himself noted—to one carved by two lovers on the trunk of a tree.

Glaser was convinced that the campaign would last no more than three months, but the "I ♥ NY" logo spread across the planet and came to be instantly identified with the city. The success of the brand and the huge revenues it generates have continued to this day, despite the derivations and countless copycats all over the world. And to think that the artist agreed to a one-time payment of a mere two thousand dollars, a sum amounting to less than that incurred by the proofs! Following the terrorist attacks of 2001, the designer reworked the logo by adding a burn

mark to the heart along with the words “More Than Ever,” and, demonstrating his affection for the city once again, did it for free. The reception of “We ♥ NYC” has been less fortunate.

The launch of this logo, which took place immediately after the Covid-19

pandemic and a couple of year's after Glaser's death with the hope of once again reversing the city's fortune, roused fierce opposition. "Instead of summing up an emotion, it belabors an image," wrote Adam Gopnik. Certain legacies remain inviolable.

▲ An oversized version of the famous logo being prepared for MoMA's reopening (August 2020)

H&M

What's Left of Broadway

"Again at eight o'clock, when the dark lanes of the Forties were lined five deep with throbbing taxicabs, bound for the theatre district, I felt a sinking in my heart. Forms leaned together in the taxis as they waited, and voices sang, and there was laughter from unheard jokes, and lighted cigarettes made unintelligible circles inside. Imagining that I, too, was hurrying towards gaiety and sharing their intimate excitement, I wished them well."

– Francis Scott Fitzgerald, *The Great Gatsby, 1925*

Fitzgerald wrote his definitive novel about the 1920s and the Jazz Age when Broadway was at its peak. The golden year was 1927, when the curtain rose on two hundred and sixty-four theatrical productions and musicals. A giddy number, especially since it pertains to a single neighborhood in a single city. The history of the Theater District, the most important in the world along with London's West End, is one of endless ups and downs.

← Aerial view of 6th Avenue and Broadway

The curtain falls at the Majestic Theatre. It is April 16, 2023, the evening of the final performance of the *Phantom of the Opera*, the longest-running musical ever in the city. It ends its run on Broadway after thirty-five years and slightly less than fourteen thousand performances. Long months of lockdown due to the pandemic, lost revenue, and the high cost of production since its reopening have multiplied its losses. The story of the disfigured composer and the beautiful soprano, adapted from Gaston Leroux's novel, had seen the arrival and departure of four hundred and fifty actors, and Andrew Lloyd Webber's score had resounded in the hall since January 26, 1988. Webber's masterpiece was not the only victim of the pandemic, of the consequent decline in tourism, and of the endemic crisis of the theatre, increasingly besieged by other forms of cultural consumption. Several other shows shared a similar fate. Broadway has certainly seen many ups and downs, but is it just a historical phase, or has an era definitively passed?

Since its origins, the term "Broadway" has nearly always been synonymous with "musical."

The first documented performance of a "musical comedy" in New York—John Gay's *Beggar's Opera*, remembered today thanks above all to Bertolt Brecht's adaptation of it in *The Threepenny Opera*—took place in 1750. A primitive performance hall had opened several decades prior on Nassau Street in Lower Manhattan.

There are forty-one theaters capable of accommodating at least five hundred spectators north of Times Square. Others, smaller in size and with fewer commercial offerings, are designated "off-Broadway"—or, if the program on the bill is even more unconventional, as "off-off-Broadway." From the *Wizard of Oz* to *Wicked*, from *West Side Story* to *Aladdin*, from *Mamma Mia!* to *Harry Potter and the Cursed Child,* Broadway musicals have set eras and guided public taste and fashion. For countless spectators, actors, and directors, a musical on Broadway is the dream of a lifetime.

The dream machine

Broadway, an old Native American trail that the Dutch renamed "Brede Wegh" or "Broad Road," runs for 13 miles at a diagonal across the island of Manhattan. At its intersection with West Twenty-Eighth Street, between Fifth and Sixth Avenues, lies an area, inconspicuous today, but which in the late nineteenth and early twentieth centuries served as the incubator of popular American culture and mass entertainment. This block, crowded at the time with publishers of sheet music, was known as **Tin Pan Alley**, a nickname arising from the great din generated by the pianos being played simultaneously by various composers. It was here that American music and a formidable recording industry were created. Over three hundred thousand pieces of popular music were registered in the first half of the twentieth century, nearly all of them prior to World War II. Most of the composers were Jews who had come over from the Old World. To this day, the best-selling single song of all time is Bing Crosby's rendition of *White Christmas*, written here in 1942 by **Irving Berlin**, a Jew from Siberia.

In 1904, the chief bureau of the *New York Times* moved to Longacre Square, where it positioned itself at the intersection of avenues that would soon become known as the "crossroads of the world." The tradition of celebrating New Year's here at midnight on December 31st

▲ Times Square

dates back more or less to that time. After spending years in the Union Square area, the active and profitable entertainment industry had spread northward in Manhattan and reached the newly renamed **Times Square**, where it was to remain permanently fixed. The district has assumed various names over the years and has expanded and contracted like a spider's web, always mirroring the unbridled ambitions of the city in its large and chaotic square and along **Forty-Second Street**.

"Times Square didn't come into being on its own: it was invented." Historian William R. Taylor examines the genesis of an urban planning project on a colossal scale: financial investment, real estate speculation, and whole new ways of attracting mass consumption: newspapers, musical productions, and theatrical spectacles. With its glittering billboards advertising products and shows that thrilled passersby, or, conversely, left them stunned, the Times Square of the 1920s became a consumerist entertainment hub. Back then, Broadway was the **Great White Way,** thanks to the lights that illuminated its signs; but with the invention of neon lighting in 1927, new electric visuals came into being. As Taylor points out, "a Broadway style that included different features, from neon lights to publicity stunts, from clothing to a manner of speaking" now worked its way into the national psyche. Broadway's sizzling nightlife offered theaters, concert halls, vaudeville with acrobats, comedians, dancers, and animal tamers. In addition to cabarets, there were burlesque clubs and fancy restaurants frequented by impresarios and gossip columnists and animated by showgirls, along with all their economic and anthropological implications.

Decline and rebirth

In the single season preceding 1929, Broadway, home to around seventy theaters, staged over two hundred and fifty productions. Thirty years later, in 1960, the *New York Times* proclaimed Forty-Second Street "the worst block in the world." The Great Depression and the rise of movies with sound dealt a severe blow to the theatre industry. Various halls were demolished or repurposed. The vibrant and unique scene of the 1920s, the one that inspired *The Great Gatsby* and the magnificent theaters designed by **Herbert J. Krapp** in a style somewhere between neoclassical and eclectic, were replaced by cheap entertainment. Once again, Times Square shed its skin to assume a decidedly kinky one full of gambling dens, striptease shows, and other sexual attractions. West Forty-second Street and Times Square gradually succumbed to a dangerous mix of crime, prostitution, and drug addiction full of sex shops, porn houses, peep shows, and seedy bars frequented exclusively by men.

To read

- Damon Runyon, ***The Best of Damon Runyon*** (1949)
- William R. Taylor, ed., ***Inventing Times Square*** (1996)
- Jerome Charyn, ***Broadway*** (2005)
- Darcy Tell, ***Times Square Spectacular*** (2007)
- Beatrice Colin, ***New York 1916*** (2011)

No longer the crossroads of the world, it became the capital of cheap sex and its excesses, and lying at the very heart of the city, open for the world to see.

The splendor of the "Great White Way" seemed lost forever. Conveying this better than any words were harrowing movies like *Taxi Driver* and *Midnight Cowboy*. Nonetheless, things began to change in the 1980s, when the city came up with ambitious projects to redevelop the neighborhood and preserve the historic structures at

▲ New Amsterdam Theatre

risk of being shattered by wrecking balls. Several theaters, including the **New Amsterdam**, the **Lyceum**, the **Ambassador**, the **Neil Simon**, and the **Palace** received protection as "New York City Landmarks." New musicals such as *Cats* and *Les Misérables* destined to make history arrived on Broadway. Mayor Rudy Giuliani's "zero tolerance" campaign of the 1990s invested particular energy into Times Square, cleaning and repurposing it. The rest is more recent history: the arrival of Disney, the renovation of the New Amsterdam Theatre, the historic home of the legendary Ziegfeld Follies, the uninterrupted success of record-breaking musicals such as *Beauty and the Beast* and, above all, *The Lion King*. All this has led to the rise of new hotels and skyscrapers and the transformation of Broadway into a distinctly tourist Disneyfied destination.

Despite facing fierce competition from Tokyo's Shibuya, the intersection at Times Square is still one of the busiest in the world. Neon has long given way to bright, high-resolution plasma screens of unprece-

◄ Broadway shows

CHICAGO
THE MUSICAL
AMBASSADOR
"CHICAGO GLITTERS HYPNOTICALLY."

dented size. Tourist traps and musicals transformed into showcases for Hollywood stars have a jarring effect, especially on those who recall the area's golden years. Walking down these streets is decidedly less dangerous today than it was in 1975, but many New Yorkers cannot hide their nostalgia for the old, run-down Broadway.

As for the present state of this creative industry, it seems that its prayers—that the immense theatrical machine return to its former, pre-2020 status as one of New York's key income generators and a golden pillar of the city's economy—have been answered.

◂ The musical *Chicago*, at the Ambassador Theatre
▾ The Naked Cowboy in Times Square

TO EXITS
4 TO 13
West
Staten Is Expwy

Sports in New York

"The New York Yankees, quite simply, are the standard by which sporting greatness is measured."

– Dick Schaap

Be they the marathon, basketball, baseball, ice hockey, or American or even European football, which is called soccer here—sports are an integral aspect of everyday life in the metropolis that never sleeps. Whatever one's preferences, they're unlikely to disappoint.

◄ The New York Marathon on the Verrazano-Narrows Bridge

Every season has its championship. The NBA's regular season runs from mid-October to April, while the playoffs go on until mid-June. The Knicks are forever seeking a title that's escaped them for decades. The Major League Baseball season with its famous Yankees—it's impossible not to run into someone with a baseball cap adorned with "N" and "Y"—runs from late March to October. The National Football League's Giants and Jets play in nearby New Jersey from September to late December. Meanwhile, the National Hockey League's Rangers and Islanders play from October to mid-June. As for soccer, one can choose which of one's overseas cousins to cheer on—City or Red Bull, whose seasons run from February to late October. Meanwhile, tennis fans won't want to miss a trip to the Billie Jean King National Tennis Center to attend a match at the U.S. Open, the final Grand Slam of the season, which takes place between late August and early September.

It's difficult to stroll along the Hudson without running into hundreds of joggers, who, regardless of the scorching sun or Arctic chill, wear special attire and pedometers on their wrists while working off the calories of yet another cream cheese-stuffed bagel or the tedium of a long day at the office. In the Big Apple, running is more than a craze—it's a manifestation of faith in the redemptive power of sports. The New York City Marathon, which takes place between late October and early November, marks the height of this philosophy; since 1970 it has become a collective annual ritual that sees tens of thousands of enthusiasts from all over the world lined up at the starting point. In 2022, nearly fifty thousand runners reached the finish line.

→ A baseball game between the Yankees and the Chicago Cubs at Yankee Stadium in the Bronx

Whether you feel like sweating through the five boroughs in sneakers, or dream of sitting in a comfortable chair at Madison Square Garden, the world's most famous sports arena, a few rows away from an iconic figure like Spike Lee, you'll not be disappointed. However, you'll need to arrange things well in advance. In New York, sports are a serious matter, and there's little space for last-minute enthusiasts, unless they're willing to pay a hefty price. Thus, it's better to take a look at the game schedule before you arrive and figure out which events you'd like to watch in person. Most importantly, be ready to enjoy yourself.

The Yankees and the Mets

Whether or not you're aware of the obscure rituals and complicated rules codified back in the 1840s by Alexander Cartwright—one of the founders

↑ Pete Alonso of the New York Mets at Citi Field in Queens

of the New York Knickerbocker Base Ball Club—going to a baseball game at **Yankee Stadium** is one of the most authentically American experiences you'll ever have. Although, in the episode in which he tries to quit drinking, Homer Simpson is amazed at how boring America's favorite sport can seem when one isn't a bit drunk, the **New York Yankees'** temple in the Bronx is a must-see not only for fans, but also for those motivated simply by curiosity. The stadium, stage for the feats of baseball's most frequently victorious team, has seen immortal icons on its turf, including Babe Ruth, king of the home run and played by John Goodman in the 1992 film *Babe*, and **Joe DiMaggio**, Marilyn Monroe's second husband, who is mentioned in the Simon & Garfunkel song *Mrs. Robinson*. It's impossible not to get carried away by the cheers of the Bleacher Creatures, the Yankees' biggest fans, whose ardent support is notorious.

The city's second team, the **Mets**, who are based in Queens, are likewise a good option for anyone wishing to enjoy a baseball game in person. Its huge apple logo that pops up after every home run, and the delicious snacks available at **Citi Field Stadium** (among the strangest, waffles with fried chicken doused in maple syrup), which can be eaten either in the stands or before entering the arena, the Mets never disappoint.

The Knicks and the Brooklyn Nets

Lit up by the more than six thousand crystals studding Marilyn Monroe's golden gauze dress as she sang "Happy Birthday, Mr. President" to JFK on the evening of May 19, 1962, the old Madison Square Garden no longer exists. The current Madison Square Garden, opened in 1968, is the stage marking the achievements of the **Knicks**, who are cherished by Spike Lee, Chris Rock, Alicia Keys, Jerry Seinfeld, and many other VIP fans, who put up with a team that seems the victim of an adverse fate. Among the most valuable brands in American sports, the Knicks—so named in honor of the "knickerbockers" worn by the early Dutch settlers on Manhattan Island—frequently end up infuriating viewers with performances that do not meet the expectations of those who lavish their love on them. But they're guaranteed to put on a good show, thanks too to the huge and very noisy scoreboard suspended over the court.

If the Knicks have spent years seeking an NBA title, which has often escaped them a second before the game ends, things aren't going any better for the city's other team, the **Brooklyn Nets,** formerly based in nearby New Jersey and today at the Barclays Center in Brooklyn. Despite having a Brooklyn-born music icon like Jay-Z, their first fan and the

For those who have never attended a live game in the United States, one of the most exhilarating aspects of the experience is watching the scoreboard, which offers support when the home team is under attack, keeps time with the fans' applause, and makes sure the public is entertained during intermissions with silly gimmicks like the famous "kiss-cam," which invites those caught in the video frame to kiss, and which has ended up in more than one romantic comedy. The one at Madison Square Garden is among the best known in the city.

designer of their logo, the team, which has been capable of attracting indisputable champions like **Kevin Durant, James Harden**, and **Kyrie Irving,** often finds itself struggling within the league. Their mediocrity has led to lower-priced and more readily available tickets than those to see their "cousins"—not an insignificant advantage for anyone dreaming of experiencing the unique atmosphere of the NBA without spending their life savings.

The Jets and Giants

A football game, another thoroughly Stars and Stripes experience, can definitely be more exciting than baseball, even if it requires going beyond the boroughs and as far as New Jersey to watch the Jets or Giants. From the moment one gets in the line outside—both teams play at the **MetLife Stadium** in East Rutherford—one is swept away by the general festive atmosphere and camaraderie that reigns at the games of the city's two teams, the **Jets** and the more famous **Giants**.

Fans hold improvised barbecues with tables full of all sorts of delicacies, prepared at home or on the spot in the parking lot. Sharing a can of beer and a plate of simple, substantial food and discussing the day's game between parked cars is a ritual repeated week after week. This is known as **tailgating** in football jargon; if you get off at a bus stop about ten minutes' walk from the stadium, you might be able to participate in it. If you arrive an hour before the game begins, you can watch the fireworks and the home team's victorious entry. Nearly as critical to the experience is the playing of the national anthem, a ritual that has been contested in recent years by many Black NFL players, whose kneeling during its performance has provoked much controversy. Between the shops, restaurants catering to all tastes, and many types of recreational activities, there is no time to get bored, and one may even end up checking the game from time to time!

10 sports memorabilia items

- The navy baseball cap with the Yankees logo in white or the classic black-on-white pinstripe uniform of America's most famous team: impressive in its 2021 version by Nike
- The Giants, known as "Big Blue," have been wearing a much-criticized red for over thirty years. On Etsy, however, one can find the team's splendid T-shirts in their original colors with a huge football helmet adorning the chest: those who see you wearing it in the stadium won't be able to withhold their emotions
- A baseball autographed by a local champion: ones signed by Babe Ruth are worth thousands of dollars
- One of the white jerseys with orange and blue piping worn by the NY Knicks in 2012. Standing out due to their retro style, they get a boost from the Number 1 that belonged to Amar'e Stoudemire, a star at the time
- A jersey belonging to the New York Cosmos, the soccer team that could deploy Pelé and Beckenbauer back in the 1970s.

Tennis, ice hockey, and soccer

If it's not the most beloved American sports that make your heart beat, then it may be a good idea to try to get a ticket to the **U.S. Open** and attend one of the many preliminary tennis matches played during the first week, which are far less excessive and easily obtainable than those in the second, when the strongest players in the ranks compete and the over seven hundred thousand fans who follow the tournament live each year gather together. The heroes of the court are **Taylor Fritz** and **Frances Tiafoe**, heirs of a school that has declined to some extent, but still lives on in the memory of the accomplishments of Agassi and Sampras in the 1990s, despite losing its primacy in the female sector to the rise of the Williams sisters.

The **Rangers** too play in Madison Square Garden, though in their case it's **ice hockey.** It's rare to experience a more boisterous atmosphere than that generated by their home fans, who get so excited during games between them and their "cousins," the Islanders, that they make the walls of the arena shake.

→ Ryan Callahan, the New York Rangers' right forward, and Anton Volchenkov, the New Jersey Devils' goalie, at Madison Square Garden

Finally, the popularity of **soccer**, a relatively new entrant in mainstream American sports, is growing rapidly, especially at the school level. World champions like the Spaniard David Villa and the Italian Andrea Pirlo both played in these parts toward the end of their careers. Today U.S. soccer no longer wants to be a destination for aged players and instead directs its focus toward youth. Certainly worth a look.

- A beautiful 1998 Rangers shirt—either white with blue sleeves and red piping or blue with white piping and red sleeves—with the stylized face of the Statue of Liberty
- The all-black, super stylish Brooklyn Nets hoodie with the logo designed by Jay-Z
- Wilson's jumbo-size tennis balls, perfect for those who collect players' autographs
- The Mets cap with the big apple

NEW YORK STOCK EXCHANGE

GRAND CENTRAL celebrates
40 YEARS RESCUED
20 YEARS RENEWED
45TH STREET

Water St
Old Dock St
SABRETT
SABRETT
HIGHMARK
HOT DOG
BEHOLD, DEFIANCE
TO FLY WHERE THEY HA
BUT WE FOUND OUR W

25

SHISH-KE-BAB
COLD BEER & SOD
LL BEEF FRANKS
CLAM STOP
KEBOB
Heineken
MAINE

THUNDERBOLT
BALLOON BUST
Prize Every Time!

7

34 St - Penn Station

ONE WAY
ONE WAY

WOK WOK
SOUTHEAST ASIAN KITCHEN

The Sacred Void

"There's no logic in the apocalypse."
– Don DeLillo, 2001

Precious events in human history have enjoyed as much media coverage as did the terrorist attacks of September 11, 2001. Only the atomic bomb, the assassination of John F. Kennedy, and, more recently, the Covid-19 pandemic have managed to equal them. The official beginning of the twenty-first century is a point of no return that still disturbs, divides, and rattles consciences. The protagonists, however, were two towers that in the less than thirty years of their existence embodied the dreams, ambitions, envy, and frustration of millions of people.

◂- Observation of the twentieth anniversary of the terrorist attack

In an interview that roused much criticism, the musician Karlheinz Stockhausen referred to the attack on the Twin Towers as a "cosmic masterpiece," albeit afterwards correcting himself by replacing the adjective with "diabolical." Some years later, the critic Achille Bonito Oliva declared that "the video of the attack had an audience that no contemporary art performance could ever equal." The words of both cast light on one of the most disturbing and consequential aspects of the culture of the new millennium: the horrible attack orchestrated by Osama bin Laden was, in fact, the most well-attended public spectacle ever staged. It took Pablo Picasso several weeks to paint the bombardment of Guernica on canvas, and he did not even need to go to the Basque country to see the massacre.

For Don DeLillo, a towering figure in American postmodern fiction, the event *flooded* the media, making everything unreal or "too real" to be absorbed. According to the author, the events of 9/11 marked a turn toward obscurantism, a move away from history and an irreversible halt to processes that were following their natural course—increasingly fluid borders, multiculturalism, and modern globalism—and of which the United States had been at the center until that moment. It was an event that sparked conflict between ideological blocs—between us and them, them and us—and one that opened the doors wide to conspiracy theories.

Ground Zero today

How does one get over the dreadful crisis of self-representation that struck Americans (and, to be honest, the entire Western world) that morning? Immediate response, defiance through height, and a

Reflecting Absence ➝

commemorative tribute were the basic coordinates. Even before the dust had settled on the ground, an endless barrage of disputes, blunders, and second thoughts poured down on the future of **Ground Zero** (a term referring to a nuclear disaster). Not until the tenth anniversary of the attacks was ***Reflecting Absence***, designed by architect Michael Arad and landscape architect Peter Walker, unveiled. Occupying the footprints of the destroyed towers, the two pools, down whose sides water cascades, literally refer to the human lives and architectural structures that no longer exist. On each anniversary of the event, two powerful vertical beams of light evoking the vanished towers and causing the dust in their path to glimmer in a deeply symbolic manner are projected into the sky. Most striking at the **9/11 Memorial Museum** *(911memorial.org)* is the oral testimony—the stories of survivors, first responders, and firefighters. One, for example, believed that he was watching an explosion of confetti, another recollected with infinite tenderness the final night that she had spent with her daughter, while yet another survivor makes visitors relive his miraculous rescue from the rubble.

The Freedom Tower, with the Oculus on the left ↑

To read

- Various authors, ***September 11th*** (2003)
- Suzanna Stephens, Ian Luna, Ron Broadhurst, ***Imagining Ground Zero*** (2005)
- Jonathan Safran Foer, ***Extremely Loud & Incredibly Close*** (2005)
- Jay McInerney, ***Good Life*** (2006)
- John Updike, ***Terrorist*** (2006)
- Mohsin Hamid, ***The Reluctant Fundamentalist*** (2007)
- Lawrence Wright, ***The Looming Tower*** (2007)
- Martin Amis, ***The Second Plane*** (2008)
- Don DeLillo, ***Falling Man*** (2008)

By comparison, the appearance of the **Freedom Tower** (One World Trade Center, officially) seems less unnerving; the core of the reconstructed World Trade Center and the country's tallest skyscraper is designed around the symbolic number 1776, which refers to both its height in feet (five hundred and forty-one meters) and the year of the U.S. Declaration of Independence. Patti Smith's tribte to the two destroyed towers may have been the most poignant of all: two blank sheets hung on the façade of her home, symbolizing the definitive loss of even the basic rules of narrating the horror, the trauma, the end of a world.

↳ The 2977 names of all the victims of the attacks are listed in a peaceful and touching manner on the bronze parapets surrounding the **Reflecting Absence** pools, set amid swamp white oaks. Around forty percent of the bodies have never been recovered, while some of the unidentified remains have been moved to the 9/11 Memorial Museum.

The signature on the new transportation hub at the heart of the World Trade Center is unmistakably that of architect Santiago Calatrava. Known as the Oculus, the white winged structure was inspired by the open one at the Pantheon, here transformed into a long narrow window between two wings.

The debris of the World Trade Center ↑

To watch

- Various directors, ***11 settembre** 2001* (2002)
- Michael Moore, ***Fahrenheit 9/11*** (2004)
- Oliver Stone, ***World Trade Center*** (2006)
- Paul Greengrass, ***United 93*** (2006)
- Stephen Daldry, ***Extremely Loud & Incredibly Close*** (2011)
- Sara Colangelo, ***Worth*** (2020)

A world in ashes

Everyone has kept the photos they snapped on that day and those following it. The firefighters and the heroic dogs. The heartrending phone calls from the skies or the towers. The courageous flight attendant or the more than two hundred people who preferred to jump into the void than face the inferno. The skeletal remains of the towers that recall the ruins of a medieval church or the cross made of steel beams that emerged from the debris. The predominant color of 9/11 is an ashen white—a dirty white emitted by tons of crumbling concrete that turned into a dangerous dust coating the polished shoes of managers and the uniforms of policemen and firefighters, while creeping into their lungs—"a bright, blinding fog, like a snowstorm on a sunny day," or, worse yet, like "the onset of a nuclear winter," as novelist Amitav Ghosh wrote several hours after the calamity.

Most likely, few people remember that before these tragic events, Islamic extremists were already plotting in the shadow of the Twin Towers. On February 26, 1993, a van packed with homemade explosives was detonated in the North Tower's underground garage. Six people were killed, and over a thousand were injured. The crater was over 196 feet in diameter. The building, however, withstood the attack, while Ramzi Yusuf, an al-Qaeda convert trained in Afghanistan, flew to Pakistan and from there to the Philippines, where he planned to blow up twelve airline jets simultaneously, assassinate John Paul II and Bill Clinton, and fly a plane right into the CIA headquarters—an operation that was to be staged in a far more spectacular way eight years later.

It was not as though American intelligence was blind—anything but that. As the turn of the millennium approached, many were convinced that Islamic terrorists would take advantage of this unprecedented opportunity to act. Their calculations, however, were wrong by about twenty months, and their predictions about the terrorists' objectives were likewise incorrect: these would not be bridges, aqueducts, or the electric grid, but rather buildings symbolizing global capitalism and America's financial power, together with the Pentagon, and either the White House or the Capitol. As everyone knows, the latter two structures (it's incredible to think that which of these was the target remains a mystery) were not hit by the kamikaze plane thanks to the heroism of several passengers, who ended up hijacking it, in turn, and crashing it in a field in Pennsylvania. The plane directed at the Pentagon, on the other hand, managed to hit the building, causing damage and casualties. After Ramzi Yusuf (again, the main author of the 1993 WTC bombing) was captured in Pakistan and extradited to the U.S. in 1995, he reportedly noted, while flying over the WTC in a helicopter, that the buildings were still standing because the organization lacked capital. It would simply be a matter of time before another attack would manage to knock them down.

Top of the world

Prior to their collapse before the eyes of the world, the height of the North (WTC 1) and the South Tower (WTC 2)—1368 and 1361 meters, respectively—had earned them the title of the world's tallest buildings for several months. Inaugurated on April 4th, 1973, they surpassed the Empire State Building in height until being surpassed by about 98 feet by Chicago's Sears Tower. The **Twin Towers** marked the first double skyscraper in the history of architecture, thus underscoring their presence and, through their "arrogance," even dwarfing the biblical Tower of Babel. From the observatory on the 107th floor of WTC 2—presumptuously called the "Top of the World"—the horizon could stretch up to 128 miles, while the chef's skills at the Windows on the World restaurant (the 106th and 107th floors of the North Tower) were barely inferior to the visual experience.

The first tribute to the structures occurred back in August 1974, when the French tightrope walker **Philippe Petit** fulfilled his lifelong dream of walking across, dancing, and lying down on a cable running between the two towers over 1312 feet above the ground. A lightning-quick performance, planned and executed in absolute secrecy without any attempt to seek permission from the police or Port Authority, the feat inspired Robert Zemeckis's movie *The Walk* (2015), starring Joseph Gordon-Levitt as Petit. Eight years later, no one would have imagined a shimmery field of wheat growing right at the foot of the towers, a strange image proposed by the Land Art pioneer **Agnes Denes**, and a powerful reflection on the ecology as well as the sentimental and economic value of the earth in an area with some of the highest real estate value on the planet.

As for critiques of the two 110-story steel-and-glass buildings (a record they held until the construction of the Burj Khalifa in Dubai), these were not always kind. Those who worked inside, for example, complained that getting down from the topmost floors took them too long as they had to change elevators multiple times and walk several hundred yards before leaving the immense square, always swept by a wind channeled by the two towers. The narrow windows of the tubular structures ("file cabinets of glass and metal," as architectural critic Lewis Mumford termed them), restricted the views from inside. In addition to the Twin Towers, the Japanese-American architect **Minoru Yamasaki** and engineer **Leslie Robertson** designed the seven connected buildings that constituted the World Trade Center. What required years to build came down in a handful of seconds. The rubble continued smoldering for ninety-nine days before the flames were fully extinguished.

Musical Venues

"New York City, I love you
New York City man
New York City, how I love you
blink your eyes and I'll be gone
just a little grain of sand."
—Lou Reed, *NYC Man*, 1996

The Big Apple has always been at the center of American music. Its streets recall pentagrams, the skyscrapers' notes suspended in the air, and the traffic a mad orchestra—as the brilliant double-bass player and composer Charles Mingus realized when inserting their rhythms into his compositions. The hundreds of spoken languages are nothing but sounds transformed into beats and movement.

← Jazz improvisation concert in Central Park

Music is the true guide in this urban world—the thread passing through every wall and ethnic group and generating the city's melting pot. Cultures and sounds lead to innovation, social and cultural changes that dictate the fashions of a constantly evolving universe. New York can satisfy any ear and passion, or simply a desire for entertainment: from hip-hop to rap, from rock to folk, blues to jazz, funk to Latin, from classical to symphonic.

Maestro **Leonard Bernstein** made the city his home. How much of New York lies in his works, or in those of the composer **Charles Ives**, who exalted it in *Central Park in the Dark*. Each district has a soundtrack that captures its mood. It is the ethnic groups, with their music and beats, that define the vibe, that fill the spaces and determine the colors of each of the neighborhoods from which Manhattan emerges, like Harlem, the cradle of African American music in New York, or Brooklyn, with its urban and angry sound.

In the **U2** video *All Because of You*, images and sounds of the Big Apple from Times Square to the Brooklyn Bridge introduce those exploring the city to the sonic and architectural delights of New York. *Angel of Harlem* is the band's splendid tribute to **Billie Holiday**, the queen of New York jazz: "New York, like a Christmas tree/Tonight this city belongs to me," sings Bono against the backdrop of a Harlem theater. There's also the New York of **John Lennon**, who was "adopted" by the city and became one of its iconic figures. He lived in the Dakota, the famous yet "cursed" building on the Upper West Side. Dedicated to him after his death, the Strawberry Fields Memorial in Central Park displays the word *"Imagine,"* solitary and powerful, at its center.

↑ Strawberry Fields Memorial in Central Park

Memory album

One can rediscover an entire archive of photographs and videos in the city's streets: the famous snapshot of **Simon & Garfunkel** on an E/F train platform, as well as their unforgettable album, *The Concert in Central Park*; **Bob Dylan** framed by Jacob Street; **The Who** of *The Kids Are Alright* sitting at 6 Morningside Drive; **Neil Young** on the cover of *After the Gold Rush* strolling down a sidewalk in Greenwich Village; **Billy Joel** on that of *An Innocent Man* sitting on a stoop at 142 Mercer Street; and **Paul Simon** on *Still Crazy After All These Days* having his picture taken on the fire escape of a building on Crosby Street.

10 music videos

- U2, ***Angel of Harlem*** (1988)
- Sting, ***Englishman in New York*** (1988)
- Public Enemy, ***Fight the Power*** (1990)
- Björk, ***Big Time Sensuality*** (1993)
- Pet Shop Boys, ***New York City Boy*** (1999)
- Ryan Adams, ***New York, New York*** (2001)
- R.E.M., ***Leaving New York*** (2004)
- Jay-Z featuring Alicia Keys, ***Empire State of Mind*** (2009)
- Lenny Kravitz, ***New York City*** (2014)
- Diana Krall, ***Autumn in New York*** (2020)

So far, we've only discussed rock and some of its greatest stars, who, thanks to multi-million sales, have disseminated the image of New York all over the world. Let's leave the lucrative and prolific world of rock behind and return for a moment to the portraits of other figures in the music world, to the photo immortalizing jazz saxophonist **Dexter Gordon** in a carriage on 59th Street and Fifth Avenue on his *Doin' Alright* album; that of soul singer **Nina Simone** sitting on a bench by Gapstow Bridge in Central Park on the cover of *Jazz as Played in an Exclusive Side Street Club*; **Harry Belafonte** at Bethesda Terrace on *Streets I Have Walked;* and, finally, the LP cover of the immortal musical ***West Side Story***, which shows the two leading characters running joyfully, hand in hand, down West 56th Street, between Ninth and Tenth Avenues, in lively Hell's Kitchen.

Inventing trends

New York, as we've already seen, has a particular affinity for music. In the 1940s, the jazz scene, with Harlem as its hub, became a global phenomenon. Be-bop along with its figures set the beat. Local venues were thronged with curious audiences eager for an intense experience. Hard bop followed on be-bop, but the "music" did not change. Record companies pushed jazz, Minton's Playhouse churned out endless great concerts, and the radio disseminated knowledge of this fascinating, smoke-filled world.

Meanwhile, Greenwich Village, on the other side of town, was changing. Shedding its reputation as a working-class neighborhood and opening up to current trends, it became the site of the new American culture. As the Beat Generation began doing its thing, the "Village" became a neighborhood of artists and musicians who performed in basements and private homes. As folk and rock began taking hold, legendary figures like **Bob Dylan** and **Joan Baez** emerged. The allure and talent of the singers/songwriters was to have a strong impact on many other artists who contributed to the exceptional character of these years. Indeed, it was after them that many others appeared on the scene, including **Paul Simon, Bruce Springsteen, Jimi Hendrix**, and **David Crosby**.

A different type of rock, more metropolitan, hard, and innovative, played in Midtown. It was here that **Andy Warhol** established his *Factory*, launching a new concept of an art open to different media, among them music. It was this world that gave origin to the **Velvet Underground**, led by **Lou Reed** and fashion model **Nico**: an avant-garde band that left an indelible mark on history and sparked many musical phenomena.

Later, in the late seventies and early eighties, came punk rock, which had its outpost in CBGB's, a venue located on the Bowery, which soon became that genre's point of reference. New wave music was also taking center stage: **Patti Smith, Blondie, Talking Heads,** and **the Ramones** were the popular artists of the time. Not to be overlooked is the fabulous "disco" scene that was its own movement after the movie *Saturday Night Fever*.

In those years, the African American response to "white" music was known as hip-hop. A social and cultural, but also—and above all—a musical lifestyle, it has now lasted for fifty years. Born in the Bronx, it spread everywhere, giving rise to phenomena such as rap, break dancing, and the sound generated by DJs in discos to this day.

The big stage

To savor the sense of history, you can start with a trip to the **Apollo Theater**, the shrine of African American music. Located in the heart of Harlem, the "Apollo" is one of the most famous theaters in the States. Founded in 1913, it went through many changes and vicissitudes before being purchased in 1991 by the state of New York, which established a foundation of the same name to run it. Here you can listen to excellent music from soul to funk and R&B, or see theater and dance performances. If you'd like to experience the emotional power of an intense gospel mass without leaving Harlem, the **Abyssinian Baptist Church** is just a few minutes' walk from the theater.

Essential for those who love pop, folk, and rock is an evening at **Brooklyn Steel**—an eighteen-hundred-seat venue on Frost Street that always offers high-level and definitely interesting programs. Another historic place worth spending an evening in is **Flushing Town Hall**. Located in Queens and erected as a municipal building in 1862, it has become a performance venue for jazz, Asian, classical, and Latin American music. Likewise steeped in history is the flamboyantly baroque **Kings Theater** in Brooklyn, which has served as a backdrop for A-list stars. Erected in 1929, it has gone through multiple lives, the latest of which began in 2015 after its restoration. It is used for top-quality live performances in a broad range of genres, from rock to folk to Caribbean music.

In the Bronx, aside from small underground locales with their intriguing sound, you shouldn't miss a chance to visit the **Lehman Center for the Performing Arts**, where you can enjoy excellent music and great ballet. On Staten Island lies another venue of notable interest: inaugurated in 1929 and renovated in 2004, the **St. George Theater** is a multidisciplinary theater, where you can hear music but also attend theatrical performances. For those who want a place pumping with adrenaline, however, there is **Terminal 5** in Hell's Kitchen: there you'll find DJs and some of the world's most famous figures in the hip-hop scene.

Next comes a whole string of smaller, more intimate venues, some of which are located in the beating heart of the Village. For jazz, there's the historic **Blue Note**, the ever-popular **Village Vanguard, Birdland**, the **Jazz Standard, Iridium**, and **Smalls Jazz Club**. If all you want are great blues, go immerse yourself in the intriguing atmosphere at **Terra Blues**.

The **Music Hall of Williamsburg** is a kind of mandatory stop: here you won't feel like a tourist and will immediately tap into the atmosphere and offerings of the multi-genre venue. For something alternative and intriguing, go to **Arlene's Grocery** on the Lower East Side, where you can listen to live sophisticated pop, rock, punk, and funk, and even take part

◄ The Apollo Theater, in Harlem

↑ Lincoln Center

Top music venues

- ***Beacon Theater:*** Historical theater on Broadway, site of many legendary concerts
- ***Carnegie Hall:*** The concert hall par excellence in which to hear classical, chamber, and contemporary music as well as jazz
- ***David Geffen Hall:*** Home of the New York Philharmonic
- ***David H. Koch Theater:*** Home of the New York City Ballet
- ***Jazz at Lincoln Center:*** The best jazz in the city
- ***Madison Square Garden:*** Known not only for sports events, but also for memorable concerts
- ***Metropolitan Opera House:*** One of the most important theaters on the planet
- ***Radio City Music Hall:*** A legend of the collective imagination

in karaoke. Finally, there's **Cafe Wha!** in the Village, a sort of temple of rock since artists like Bob Dylan, Jimi Hendrix, and Bruce Springsteen got their start there.

Radio City Music Hall →

RADIO CITY
MUSIC HALL
RADIO CITY
MUSIC HALL
Music Hall
RADIO CITY
Music Hall
RADIO CITY
CONAN GRAY
MARCH 16
MITSKI
DANIEL HABIF
MARCH 25
SNOH AALEGRA
MARCH 26 & 29

Welcome to the
WTC
LYNNE YUN
SOKOKI STUDIOS

A Painted Concrete Jungle

"New York calls to graffiti writers like a dirty old lighthouse. We all want to prove ourselves here."

– Banksy, 2013

New York possesses an irresistible allure for artists across the globe; it is a place of devout pilgrimage for creative people of all sorts. These days, international brands compete over artists, while public entities commission colossal and multimedia works. The gentrification of Street Art has reached an advanced stage, but the path out of anonymity and illegality has been a long and fascinating one.

← Mural Project: graffiti at the construction site of Two World Trade Center

Urban Art, writing, graffiti, tags, murals, Aerosol Art, stickers, stencils, posters. . . . There's an entire semantic universe that must be discovered for anyone wishing to approach Street Art knowledgeably. Little more than fifty years lie between the first cryptic tags scrawled with magic markers on the walls of the Bronx and the gigantic artistic enterprises that have overtaken the city's buildings today and make eyes pop thanks too to new, sophisticated immersive and sensorial technologies. Half a century has literally capsized our way of looking at and perceiving street art, its creators, and the very meaning of the metropolis. Moving away from the concerns of the seventies and eighties—illegality, vandalism, decrepitude, urban decorum, exorbitant cleaning costs—we have set aside suspicion and prejudice to fully embrace the genre within the art system and now provide guided tours of cult sites driven by our conviction that Street Art is the most widespread artistic movement on the planet.

Surprising, ephemeral, already gone

Nearly 7 million dollars. This was the historical mega sum granted to twenty-one artists after their graffiti was wiped out in a single night at **5Pointz,** one of the temples of New York Street Art until late 2013. The run-down industrial complex in Long Island City, Queens, became a training ground for hundreds of artists, a place of endless attraction for tourists and the curious.

Many sites with Street Art no longer exist, but this is intrinsic to the movement's ephemeral and transitory nature. Such was the case of **11 Spring Street**, in Nolita, a one-story-tall open-air gallery. For years, artists covered it with spray paint, posters, and stencils,

→ A 2006 snapshot of the Graffiti Hall of Fame in East Harlem

unimpeded for the most part by the authorities. Reporting its destruction on December 14, 2006, the *New York Times* wrote that it was "as if someone had told devotees of Picasso's *Demoiselles d'Avignon* or Matisse's *Dance* that the Museum of Modern Art had changed hands and would soon close its doors for real estate redevelopment, and that all the art inside would vanish as part of the deal." Devoured by the advance of urban redevelopment, real estate speculation, and housing demands (always for luxury apartments), such places are forever changing.

There are also sites initiated with a deliberately ephemeral purpose, such as the grand **Two World Trade Center Murals Project at Ground Zero**, which will remain in place until the conclusion of construction at the site. What's left today from the pioneering era of Street Art is the **Graffiti Hall of Fame in East Harlem**, a long public wall launched in

1980 by Ray Rodriguez, better known by his pseudonym Sting Ray, and updated every year, when each artist selected can pour forth their own style. In the heart of this African American neighborhood is a series of paintings done on **Harlem Hospital** that enable us to travel back in time to the era of the Great Depression and the Muralist movement.

In New York, the streets speak

Ellis Island is where the American dream took shape for over 12 million men, women, and children. An itinerary through the sites of New York Street Art, which is chronologically impossible, could symbolically begin here. Longevity is not a distinctive feature of graffiti, which sometimes lasts just long enough to be shot in a photograph. Works that appear one morning may be gone or vandalized a few days later. Others, fortunately, survive over time. It's better to let oneself zigzag at will and stand amazed at every corner. The anonymous French artist **"JR"** left a powerful message on the abandoned hospital complex at Ellis Island. The faces of immigrants, reproduced from original photographs unearthed in the archives, scrutinize and interrogate, striking one head-on. JR's other collages in New York survive only in photographic documents, but their deeper significance lives on. There's not a borough in New York that hasn't been marked by graffiti and Street Art. In the last half century the creative use of the wall and the street has generated both tiny signs and monumental works, fed on current events and social issues, paid homage to great figures and everyday people, and distilled material from the entire flow of history: Native Americans, Audrey Hepburn, AIDs, Muhammed Ali, ecology, Black Lives Matter. . . .

The concentration of graffiti and murals in the circle comprising **Soho**, the **Bowery**, the **Lower East Side,** and **Chinatown** in Lower Manhattan is impressive. To get a proper sense of the situation these days, one needs to shoot down to the intersection of Houston and the Bowery to see the

↑ The Mona Lisa of Williamsburg

Bowery Wall, a concrete wall blessed by Keith Haring and an experimental platform ever since for urban art that's been entrusted to various artists. The next stop is the **Meatpacking District** and the **High Line**, then Brooklyn, particularly **Williamsburg**, considered one of the meccas of the genre, where a modern Mona Lisa greets visitors. From there one can go as far as **Bushwick** in northeastern Brooklyn, the epicenter of the most flamboyant Street Art and home to the city's largest Hispanic community. Here, a substantial group of street artists under the leadership of Joe Ficalora known as the **Bushwick Collective** has literally revolutionized the former working-class neighborhood since 2011, making it explode with color, narratives, and life and transforming it from an off-limits area into a tourist destination.

There's an open hunt for **Banksy**'s ironic messages like that of the Hammer Boy—a stencil of a child hammering a fire hydrant on the Up-

↑ Obey's *Long Live the Revolution* (painted over in 2020), conceived as a tribute to his daughter Vivienne

To consult

- artsandculture.google.com/partner/street-art-nyc
- citizenm.com/mosa/overview
- findmasa.com
- instagram.com/thebushwickcollective
- streetart.withgoogle.com
- streetartcities.com
- streetartnyc.org

per West Side—among the skyscrapers, avenues, and parks. As one's vision sharpens, one will notice among buildings the stylized long-legged men by the English artist **Stik**, the huge black-and-white creatures of the Belgian artist **ROA**, and the iconic faces of the Neapolitan Jorit (easily recognizable because their cheeks are marked with two red stripes). And one can also indulge in wonder at the texts posted by Shepard Fairey, better known by his pseudonym **Obey**, the undisputed pioneer of sticker art.

↳ The exuberant colors of **Eduardo Kobra** are easily recognizable on the walls of Manhattan and Brooklyn. The Brazilian street artist's gigantic works are infused with social messages and "snapshots" of history, *pop culture*, and art figures, from Anne Frank and Vivian Maier to Einstein, Michael Jackson, and the heroic firefighters of 9/11. Likewise from Brazil are the duo **Os Gêmeos** (Otavio and Gustavo Pandolfo), famous by now for their melancholic, poetic, and subtly surreal characters with faces of a distinct bright yellow hue—the color, they claim, in which they usually dream.

← Os Gêmeos's *Break-dancer* appeared on a building on Second Avenue in 2015.

The Women of Street Art

A tough, dangerous art, an unrestrained, wild, unconventional lifestyle. Street Art would seem to be exclusively male territory, yet a significant percentage of graffiti artists are actually women, many of whom work in New York. The first of these artists to become famous was **Lady Pink**, an Ecuadorian who was already an active writer in the late 1970s. Sandra Fabara (her real name) has used graffiti to advocate for equal rights and equal opportunities in socially conscious messages of a large format done in loud colors. The black and queer American activist **Tatyana Fazlalizadeh**, who launched the famous "Stop Telling Women to Smile" poster campaign, focuses on the issue of harassment on the street. Recognizable for a style that combines oriental features with Pop Art is the Japanese artist **Lady Aiko**, who landed on the streets of New York after fleeing the macho culture of her country. The burlesque style of **Miss Van** is softer, more subtly erotic, while the huge-eyed mythical female creatures of **Alice Mizrachi** seem to be ancestral prototypes.

From tags to spray cans: writers and graffiti artists

It was at the tail end of the 1960s when groups of Puerto Rican and African American youth from the city's poorest neighborhoods (especially the South Bronx) began covering the walls of run-down buildings with a signature and number in stylized letters. Thus came about the first tags, done with thick indelible markers, and the first **writers**. They generally joined small crews and took on code names: **Julio 204** (a kid from 204th Street), **Junior 161**, and **Taki 183**, a seventeen-year-old Greek-American youth to whom the *New York Times* dedicated its first article on the subject in July 1971.

A phenomenon initially limited to the ghetto, writing spread like wildfire, and tags began taking over walls and out-of-the-way public places: above all, subway cars and stations. The tags of a single writer would multiply; grow larger; and appear in extreme, difficult-to-reach locations that showed their contempt for danger. The style became more refined and the lettering ever more elaborate and captivating with the introduction of color, the "bubble style," "bar (square) letters," and three-dimensionality. Writers eventually became graffiti artists, affirming their individuality with a mark that brought them visibility in a race for fame based on signs comprehensible only to other members of the same metropolitan tribe: the password was "getting up," that is, emerging. From walls they moved on to subway cars and from markers to spray cans: the signature could now travel throughout the city, spreading its message.

In the late 1970s, the MTA began using a costly acid-based method known as the "buff system" to clean subway cars—in vain, of course. "It's a sign we've lost control," declared the president of the MTA in 1984 just as the city plunged into a nearly unprecedented urban crisis. At least six hundred and fifty writers had been identified by 1972, the year of the first underground exhibition. This was the first time that a low form of expression had been elevated to the status of art and even exhibited in a gallery.

◂ Lady Pink at work at Casita Maria, in the Bronx (2019)

To watch

- Tony Silver, ***Style Wars*** (1983)
- Charlie Ahearn, ***Wild Style*** (1983)
- Julian Schnabel, ***Basquiat*** (1996)
- Edo Bertoglio, ***New York Beat Movie (Downtown 81)*** (2000, but filmed in 1980-81)
- Adam Bhala Lough, ***Bomb the System*** (2002)
- Francesco Mazza, ***Graffiti a New York*** (2015)
- Roger Gastman, ***Wall Writers: Graffiti in Its Innocence*** (2016)
- Oren Jacoby, ***Shadowman*** (2017)
- Cedric Godin, ***X art*** (2018)
- Ryan Dowling, ***Duality: A Graffiti Story*** (2022)

To read

- Duccio Dogheria, ***Street Art*** (2015)
- Jaime Rojo and Steven P. Harrington, ***Street Art New York*** (2021)
- Alessandra Mattanza, ***Le grandi artiste della Street Art*** (2022)
- Simon Armstrong, ***Street Art*** (2022)

The transition from the underground to the mainstream was quick: ten years later, graffiti was inducted into the art world at the international exposition Documenta 7 in Kassel. It was no longer necessary to dart around tunnels with bated breath in the dark of night, risking fines or even arrest: emancipation had arrived. Gallerists began competing for writers and graffiti artists. This was the era of **A-One, Futura 2000, Lee Quiñones, Donald Baechler, Rammelzee,** and **Lady Pink**, as well as Keith Haring and Jean-Michel Basquiat.

Precious little is left of **Keith Haring** on the walls of New York, but a trek to the area between Second Avenue and the Harlem River Drive is obligatory for those who still wish to be surprised at the thick lines and unmistakable stylized shapes—forever fresh—that hover between tribal art and cartoon. *Crack is Wack* (1986) is an outcry against the spread of drugs in the years when the city fell prey to a veritable epidemic, the very same one that in 1988 snatched away the child prodigy **Jean-Michel Basquiat** at the tender age of 27—that same cursed age at which so many talented artists have been extinguished—

→ Superman, Batman, and Wonder Woman wearing masks in Chelsea during the Covid-19 pandemic (2020)

and who had made his debut as Samo (a twist on the phrase "the same old shit" in reference to pot). Basquiat's works, in which crudely painted figures are mixed with texts and signs, cannot be found on the street, but only in galleries, since he was the first to transfer the message from walls to canvas, from streets to exhibitions.

By the late 1980s, Street Art had entered institutions from the Museum of Modern Art and the Whitney Museum of American Art to the Brooklyn Museum and the Museum of Street Art/MOSA on the Bowery, in addition to countless specialized galleries. Does this mark a betrayal of the original message? Its commodification? For some, it signifies an inevitable loss of the innovative energy of Street Art, of its free, wild, gratuitous, illegal quality. For others, it represents the inevitable evolutionary process of an art born in the ghetto, nurtured between subway cars and walls, and today "instagrammed" by tourists and adored by brands, without, however, abandoning its role as a powerful driver of social change.

SABRETT
WE'RE ON A ROLL !!!
HOT
HOT DOG
SHISH KEBAB
ITALIAN SAUSAGE
CHICKEN KEBAB
SHISH KEBAB
HALAL FOOD
PRETZEL
ITALIAN SAUSAGE
HOT SAUSAGE
KNISHES
HOT DOG
CHICKEN KEBAB
CHILI DOG
SODA
WATER
SNAPPLE
GATORADE
SABRETT

World Cuisine

"Your body is not a temple, it's an amusement park. Enjoy the ride."

– Anthony Bourdain

The shocking revelations in *Kitchen Confidential* (published in 2000, but still quite relevant), the legendary memoir of Anthony Bourdain, the irreverent but honest insider at New York's restaurant kitchens, simply add spice to a gastronomic scene that is constantly reinventing and redefining itself. As in many other sectors, the buzzwords of New York's restaurant industry are "experiment," "astonish," and "flaunt," with "feed" only as an afterthought. For that reason, it's better . . . to enjoy the ride than think about one's diet (or wallet).

◂ Any time is good for a hot dog or pretzel

As the number of Michelin-starred venues continues to rise year after year, the Big Apple solidifies its status as the gastronomic mecca of the States, and beyond. Almost all of these are concentrated in Manhattan, but trendy Brooklyn is beginning to vaunt its aces. Albeit something of a cliché, in New York City the most hardcore foodies can truly tour the five continents. Do you feel like eating Korean, Caribbean, Greek, Puerto Rican, Scandinavian, Palestinian, Uzbek, Bolivian? Are you "simply" a vegan or a hardcore raw food fan, a champion of urban agriculture or an adventurous person who dares to try insects and animal offal? Would you like to enjoy a dinner blindfolded or even naked? Dine on a boat or a panoramic rooftop? It's really difficult to keep up with trends, but any desire can be satisfied here. The important thing is to plan, make reservations, and have fun—like a true New Yorker. In this chapter, however, we will focus especially on "typical" New York cuisine, assuming that such a thing even exists.

The immigrant's suitcase

The first restaurant on American soil in the modern sense of the term opened its doors on William Street in Lower Manhattan in 1827. The menu at **Delmonico's** (the name belonged to that of two brothers from Ticino) was a hundred pages long, and its wine cellar boasted no fewer than sixteen thousand bottles. The progenitor of all chic New York venues closed down in 1923, though was later reborn. In the meantime, high-class restaurants offering European food sprung up like mushrooms, side by side with more affordable food stands and clubs. To this day, the city's gastronomic fare, albeit updated and far improved, adheres to this model—one capable of satisfying all budgets.

Italians, Eastern European Jews, the Chinese and Germans: an amalgam of old-time gastronomic traditions that still feeds the arteries of the metropolis, fat-laden and forever dying for the thrill of novelty. It is in the triangulation of Naples, New York, and Italy that **pizza** as we know it today was born. A dish of Mediterranean and Neapolitan origin, pizza became unbelievably popular in the States thanks to the Neapolitan emigrants of the nineteenth and twentieth centuries. After undergoing a transformation, it returned to Italy via U.S. soldiers during World War II, where it took on its present form. The pizza chef Gennaro Lombardi opened **Lombardi's**, the first American pizzeria, in Little Italy in 1905. From that time on, American pizza—a triangular slice with a thin, crunchy crust and an equally thin layer of sauce, and eaten folded in half—or else its "Neapolitan" version, enjoys ever more enthusiastic acclaim in its innumerable variants and garnishes.

It seems that the craze for **hot dogs**, by contrast, was initiated by a German immigrant, Charles Feltman. Lending proof to the hypothesis that the student often surpasses their master, it was the Polish-American Nathan Handwerker who guaranteed its commercial success by advertising his sau-

10 iconic New York food items

- ***Bagel:*** the legendary ring of bread dough, first boiled, then baked in the oven and coated with poppy or sesame seeds, and finally stuffed with smoked salmon and fresh cream cheese
- ***Brownies:*** soft and irresistible blocks of baked chocolate dough
- ***Donuts:*** the sweet, deep-fried pastries beloved by Homer Simpson, glazed or filled with cream or jelly
- ***Eggs Benedict***: poached eggs and bacon on an English muffin, served with hollandaise sauce . . . a legendary dish, (possibly) created for a customer at the Waldorf Astoria to alleviate his hangover
- ***Hamburger:*** the great American street food classic available in infinite versions—cheeseburgers, veggie burgers, double burgers—as varied as the chef's imagination and individual preferences
- ***Muffins:*** soft and fluffy mini cakes, garnished according to taste
- ***New York cheesecake:*** the local version includes—in addition to cream cheese—cookie crumbs and vanilla
- ***Pancakes:*** topped with fresh fruit, maple syrup, and butter
- ***Pastrami:*** a must-have Kosher delicacy
- ***S'mores:*** tantalizing marshmallows between two chocolate-coated cookies

↑ Junior's Restaurant, famous for its cheesecake

sages on huge billboards, cutting their price by half, and launching a contest for hot-dog eaters destined to long-term success (the former world record was broken in 2020 by Joey Chestnut, who gulped down seventy-five hot dogs in scarcely ten minutes). Still in business today, **Nathan's Famous**, along the shore of Coney Island, is one of those venues that have left its mark on the history of American food culture. Yeah, but why, in fact, are these soft sandwich rolls stuffed with frankfurters, pickles, sauerkraut, onions, and mustard called "hot dogs"? There are various theories, but it seems plausible that "dog" comes from the resemblance of the sausage to a dachshund, a dog that is likewise German, while "hot" comes from the fact that it is hot when served.

The legacy of kosher cooking is enormous; the number of recipes that have been passed down by the Ashkenazi tradition is incalculable. The standard bearers include the **bagel**, the incredibly successful ring of

→ Pastrami sandwiches

bread that can be found in any New York bakery, and **pastrami**, salted and seasoned beef brisket eaten between two slices of rye bread. Nonetheless, the list is extensive: from the unleavened dumplings in broth known as **matzo ball soup**, to **latkes**, an Ashkenazi alternative to conventional French fries, and from the oven-baked rolls known as **bialys**, to **pierogi**, essentially pan-fried potato ravioli. The list gets ever longer and contaminated by unconventional trends.

The culinary history of New York therefore consists of a long series of borrowings and imaginative reworkings. Each ethnic group has contributed to the creation of this gastronomic laboratory, unique to this world, and to its grand menu, which changes from day to day but always includes dishes from Mexico, Vietnam, Japan, France, the Middle East, and other states of the Union. This explains why **New York's 10 emblematic dishes** (page 127) listed in the box below, include very few invented in the Big Apple, though all have contributed to its iconic status even in the dining room.

↳ The largest Chinese community in the United States is also home to a huge number of immigrants from other Asian nations, including Vietnam. One can take a unique journey that touches on all the areas of East Asia, above all at the dining table, with their exhilarating flavors and smells, in traditional food joints, trendy restaurants, and bubble tea shops—not only in touristy Chinatown, but also and especially in other ethnic outposts scattered around the city, including some in Brooklyn and Queens.

↑ Peking Duck at a restaurant in Chinatown

↑ The original Manhattan cocktail, garnished with flambéed orange rind

First, a cocktail

New York knows how to be self-referential even in the art of mixology. Many famous cocktails are named after one of the five boroughs. The aristocratic **Manhattan** (rye, red vermouth, a drop of angostura, and a cherry), for example, boasts a history a century and a half long. More recent is **Long Island Iced Tea** (vodka, tequila, rum, gin, Coke, and sweet and sour mix), invented on the Island in 1972, and offering a whiff of summer or possibly Prohibition, when a similar cocktail had been passed off as an iced tea beverage.

We've left the Martini (gin and vermouth) for last—a cocktail so glorified by the writers, directors, and producers of TV shows that it has held the status of legend since its inception (though without diminishing that of the whiskey-based **Old Fashioned**). Nikita Khrushchev called the Martini "the deadliest U.S. weapon." Whether traditional, dry, or extra dry, this supremely elegant and transparent cocktail, served in its iconic thin-stemmed glass and garnished solely with a lemon twist or olive, should be savored with utter equanimity.

Green markets and urban farms

Cider, exotic mushrooms, kimchi, berries, Mexican herbs, edible flowers, bison meat, rainbow trout, emu eggs, you name it. . . . Among the vital components of the city's gastronomic scene are the **fruit and vegetable**

markets that sell vegetables, meats, and many other products directly from regional producers. About fifty in all (though the number is growing) are scattered throughout various neighborhoods. The most famous and popular—with around 140 vendors—is still the one in **Union Square**, but even the smaller ones promise genuine discoveries. These are definitely worth a visit, if for no other reason than to taste of something delicious, or to observe, with a touch of curiosity, trendy health-obsessed New Yorkers and famous chefs looking for fresh products for their amazing culinary creations.

If green markets allow residents to enjoy food grown a few miles from home, **community gardens** delve even deeper into the concept of sustainability, allowing the community to participate personally in the production of their own food and fostering a connection with nature even in this highly urbanized environment. Aside from school-related and general gardens, there are over five hundred and fifty community gardens in the city. In the early 1970s, the **Green Guerillas**, artist-activists in a city struck by a deep financial and identity crisis, began dropping ready-to-take-root "seed bombs" and thus brought abandoned lots back to life.

Even if constantly threatened by real estate speculation, or located in the most disadvantaged communities, tiny green oases between concrete and large urban farms—some perched on the roofs of buildings—help transform neighborhoods, increase biodiversity (simply by attracting pollinating insects), reduce imports, add to residents' direct knowledge of nature, and enhance their social life.

◂ The Christmas market at Union Square

Movies and TV Series Shot on Location

"In Hollywood, actors learn to act from watching television. In New York, people learn to act by walking down the street."

– Sidney Lumet

The IMDb-Internet Movie Database lists two hundred and sixty-seven feature films whose titles contain the city's name—from *New York, New York* (1977) starring Liza Minnelli and Robert De Niro, to *Autumn in New York* (2000) with Richard Gere and Winona Ryder, and *Gangs of New York* (2002) with Leonardo DiCaprio, Daniel Day-Lewis, and Cameron Diaz. The earliest such movie on record is *The Lure of New York*, which dates to 1913.

← Woody Allen before the Coney Island cyclone on the movie set of *Annie Hall*, 1977

This number does not include TV series and miniseries (of which there are 274), TV movies (145), or screenplays (at least 4,455!), or video clips, short films, and podcasts. If we then add all the movies that are set in New York but don't contain its name in the title (an inestimable number—we're talking here about dozens of productions occurring on a daily basis), we begin to understand why every corner of New York City seems to have popped out of a screen, and why even those who have never set foot here are perfectly familiar with its red brick buildings, fire escapes, yellow cabs, and steaming manhole covers.

In this chapter we won't talk about Woody Allen or the unforgettable shot of the Queensboro Bridge in *Manhattan* (1979) or about the piercing chords of George Gershwin's *Rhapsody in Blue*. Nor will we discuss the extent to which King Kong's climb up the Empire State Building in the 1933 cult film inspired legions of science-fiction and disaster-movie directors. Remember the scene when the skyscraper gets destroyed in *Independence Day* (1996)? And the one in which *Godzilla* (1988) scales the Chrysler Building? We will not even discuss Meg Ryan's simulation of an orgasm at Katz's Delicatessen on the Lower East Side, in *When Harry Met Sally* (1989) or about Audrey Hepburn, the inimitable icon of sophistication, in *Breakfast at Tiffany's* (1961).

As for the beloved series *Friends* (1994-2004), apart from the exterior of the building shown at least once per episode—you'll find it in Greenwich Village, between Grove and Bedford Streets—all the interiors were shot on the West Coast. The same goes for

→ The Manhattan Bridge in Dumbo, the scene set used in the poster for *Once Upon a Time in America* (p. 138)

Will & Grace (1998-2020) and *Suits* (2012-2019); the latter, despite its look, was shot almost entirely in Toronto.

Those that follow, therefore, are some intimate clips of New York cinematography drawn from feature films, and TV series, in which, aside from serving as a magnificent backdrop, the city plays a major role.

Midnight Cowboy (1969)

The sordid side of city life and male prostitution are the subjects of British director John Schlesinger's masterpiece. Catapulted from rural Texas to the Big Apple, Joe Buck (John Voight) is confronted with a series of (mis)adventures and scams until he meets Rico Rizzo (Dustin Hoffman),

an outcast and physically disabled petty thief, with whom he establishes his only true bond, albeit in the mutual solitude of their two lives. The movie displays an unforgettable slice of the **Times Square** that once was but has now vanished. Fun fact: *Midnight Cowboy* was the first censored feature film to win an Oscar for best picture, as well as those for directing and adapted screenplay.

Taxi Driver (1976)

In terms of subject matter, *Taxi Driver* is a film that penetrates the city's (filthy and congested) streets. From **Times Square** to **Columbus Circle**, from **Hell's Kitchen** to **Broadway** theaters and the **St. Regis Hotel**, the streets of Manhattan unfold before both our eyes and those of the protagonist, the taxi driver Travis Bickle, who is weighed down by loneliness, insomnia, and mounting anger in a violent and run-down city—a character that Robert De Niro immortalized under the direction of Martin Scorsese.

Once Upon a Time in America (1984)

Is there any shot of New York City—save that of the Queensboro Bridge in *Manhattan*—more stunning than that of the **Manhattan Bridge** immortalized in this feature film (a fitting term for a movie nearly four hours long) by Sergio Leone? You can go see it for yourself from the intersection of Washington and Water Street in Dumbo (Brooklyn) and recall the scene of the confrontation between the Noodles gang (which includes Robert De Niro) and Bugsy while imagining the splendid poster before your eyes and listening to Ennio Morricone's score on your headphones.

➔ The *Ghostbusters* fire station in Tribeca

Ghostbusters (1984)

We had a hard time deciding on a kids' movie from the '80s or '90s. The choice, which is vast, ranges from *Big* (1988), in which Tom Hanks plays the gigantic piano at FAO Schwartz (which, unfortunately, no longer exists in that place) with his feet, to *Home Alone 2: Lost in New York* (1992), in the course of which Macaulay Culkin encounters the city's celebrities parading from the **Plaza Hotel** down to **Rockefeller Center**, and from the **World Trade Center** and the **Battery** up to **Central Park**. In the end, we chose *Ghostbusters* along with its most memorable location, the headquarters of the ghost catchers (Bill Murray and Dan Aykroyd among them), an actual red-brick firehouse, the **Hook & Ladder Company 8** (dating to 1903), still active today and constantly photographed at 14 North Moore Street in Tribeca. The interior, on the other hand, is in . . . Los Angeles. Of course, we can't overlook **Columbia University** and the **New York Public Library**. Yet, here too, some of the interiors were those of the Central Library . . . in L.A.!

Wall Street (1987)

The temple of the money god is one of the sets in which the greedy ("but virtuous") humanity of Gordon Gekko (Michael Douglas) and the ambition of Bud Fox (Charlie Sheen) operate. The movie, directed by Oliver Stone, crystallized forever the prototype of the '80s yuppie. In addition to the **New York Stock Exchange**, it features two other cult places of the time: the **21 Club**, the city's most famous speakeasy, which hosted an endless stream of political, entertainment, and culture personalities until its closure in 2020, and **Tavern on the Green** along with its iconic Central-Park-facing Crystal Room. As for the Stock Exchange, even Stone was accorded only 45 minutes to shoot the several *Wall Street* scenes in there. The building and the *Charging Bull* appear in countless movies: we remind you of just one of many other unmissable masterpieces likewise directed by a New Yorker, Martin Scorsese: *The Wolf of Wall Street* (2013).

Do the Right Thing (1989)

Bedford-Stuyvesant, Brooklyn, was the open-air set—still partly recognizable today—for Spike Lee's colorful masterpiece *Do the Right Thing*. The tension between Italian Americans and African Americans, which emerges little by little until the tragic epilogue on a sweltering summer day, forms the plot for a line-up of memorable characters, from the pizza delivery man (played by the director himself) to Radio Raheem, who goes around all day with a huge stereo on his shoulders blasting Public Enemy's *Fight the Power* (Spike Lee directed the video clip for that too), all the way down to Smiley, a stuttering youth who tries to sell everybody photos of Malcolm X and Martin Luther King.

The 25th Hour (2002)

The epic shot of the Manhattan Bridge by Sergio Leone makes a deliberate comeback, albeit with the addition of **Carl Schurz Park** on the East River, with its long benches facing the Roosevelt Island lighthouse. It is here that the day begins and ends for the main character and his dog, and the rubble of **Ground Zero**, destroyed less than a year earlier, is replaced by two cones of light projecting into the sky. This was among the first feature films to show the wounds of the 9/11 attack. The compelling plot was based on that of a novel by David Benioff (though written before that date), and directed by Spike Lee. (The two rewrote the screenplay to match the power of the historical moment.) Playing Monty Brogan, Edward Norton gives life to an unforgettable character. Twenty-four hours before checking into prison, where he will serve a seven-year sentence for drug dealing, he decides to spend one last night of freedom in the city in the company of his two best friends and his girlfriend—a night in which anything can happen, including an extra hour. Indeed, everything does happens, even though later it becomes bitterly clear that no one can escape their destiny.

Spider-Man (2002, 2004, 2007)

According to Federico Pagello, one of the genre's leading experts, the Spider-Man trilogy directed by Sam Raimi "is undoubtedly the most explicit

10 not-to-be-missed treats

- ***New York Stories*** (1989), directed by Martin Scorsese, Francis Ford Coppola, and Woody Allen
- ***Léon*** (1994), directed by Luc Besson
- ***Mad Men*** (2007-2015), TV series, various directors
- ***Synecdoche, New York*** (2008), directed by Charlie Kaufman
- ***Frances Ha*** (2012), directed by Noah Baumbach
- ***Inside Llewyn Davis*** (2013), directed by Joel and Ethan Coen
- ***Sully*** (2016), directed by Clint Eastwood
- ***Succession*** (2018-2023), TV series, various directors
- ***Unorthodox*** (2020), TV miniseries directed by Maria Schrader
- ***Fran Lebowitz—Pretend It's a City*** (2021), directed by Martin Scorsese

To read

- Claudia Hellmann and Claudine Weber-Hof, ***Location*** (2006)
- Federico Pagello, ***Grattacieli e superuomini*** (2010)
- Barbara Boesplfug and Bea trice Billon, ***The Film Lover's New York*** (2014)
- Stella Cervasio and Alessandro Vaccaro, ***Grand Central Dream*** (2021)
- Jason Bailey, ***Fun City Cinema*** (2022)

Bethesda Fountain in Central Park

To consult

- afi.com
- imdb.com
- movie-locations.com/places/usa/nyc.php
- onthesetofnewyork.com

praise of the role of New York in the cinematic superhero vein. No other movie (and perhaps no comic series) has devoted as much space to this city." Virtually all of its highlights appear in it: from the **Flatiron Building** to **Columbia University**, from **St. Patrick's Cathedral** to the **American Museum of Natural History**—the list is virtually endless. An excellent refresher for anyone about to set foot in the city, it's a binge-watching event that extends to all things related to Batman, the Fantastic Four, X-Men, Daredevil, and the Avengers.

Angels in America (2003)

Although many scenes in this TV miniseries, based on Tony Kushner's eponymous play, were shot indoors and in hospital rooms, the finale features the angel of **Bethesda Fountain** at the heart of **Central Park**. (Note: According to a 2020 report, Central Park—with at least five hundred thirty-two movies filmed on its grounds—is the most frequently filmed location in the world.)

The series is set in 1985, just as AIDS surfaces in the city, which is about to be overwhelmed. The disease is already upsetting the equilibrium of the gay community, as well as ties and friendships within it and beyond. The epilogue consists of a monologue delivered by Prior after he discovers that he has been infected: "This disease will be the end of many of us, but not nearly all, and the dead will be commemorated and will struggle on with the living, and we are not going away. We won't die secret deaths anymore. The world only spins forward. We will be citizens. The time has come. Bye now. You are fabulous creatures, each and every one. And I bless you: More Life. The Great Work Begins." The fountain recalls the biblical pool of Betzaeta in Jerusalem, where Jesus healed a paralytic—a parallel packed with meaning and hope. And the grand exit by the leading actors (Meryl Streep among them) up the stairs of **Bethesda Terrace** leaves movie-goers in tears.

Birdman (2014)

Making just sixteen cuts in the entire film (nearly two hours long), the Mexican director Alejandro González Iñárritu shot a very long, slow scene that unfolds in a continuous and hypnotic flow among the theater studios and the streets of **Times Square** and **Broadway**, over which the main character dreams of flying. This is a highly complex cinematic achievement in which the camera seems to endlessly follow Michael Keaton (who played in two of Tim Burton's Batman movies) as he desperately tries to escape the character who has made him famous, the superhero Birdman.

↳ The poster for *Joker* (2019) is effective, but the actual scene is even more so. Todd Phillips makes Joaquin Phoenix (aka Arthur Fleck) dance to the tune of Gary Glitter's *Rock and Roll Part 2* while descending a steep staircase. That staircase does exist and is located in the Bronx, more specifically, in Highbridge.

↳ How many times have we seen her go down those stairs on her way out to conquer the city? Carrie Bradshaw, however, does not actually live in the apartment at 245 East 73rd Street on the Upper East Side, but rather at Perry Street, in the heart of the West Village. That is, as long as she remains single, because after marrying Mr. Big, she moves to 1010 Fifth Avenue. Some numerical data give just a vague idea of the breadth of the *Sex & The City* phenomenon: the series consisted of ninety-four episodes over six seasons (1998-2004), inspired two films, and included four protagonists: Carrie, Miranda, Charlotte, and Samantha. Besides Manhattan, of course.

Diasporas

"Let America be the dream the dreamers dreamed
Let it be that great strong land of love
Where never kings connive nor tyrants scheme
That any man be crushed by one above."

– Langston Hughes, 1963

New York City is one of the most ethnically diverse cities in the world with immigrant communities from every corner of the globe. African American, Chinese, and Jewish New Yorkers are three groups that represent some of New York's oldest diaspora communities. Every ten years the census redraws the map indicating the movement and distribution of inhabitants in different neighborhoods, and the political system has to deal with the change in electoral votes in each of them. One thing, however, that binds these three groups together is their experience as diasporas, with the dual meaning of having dispersed and having spread their own seed.

← Women on the Brooklyn Bridge celebrating Falun Dafa World Day, a Chinese spiritual practice

In contrast to the others, African Americans were the only ones brought to the United States against their will. In 2020, journalist Nikole Hannah-Jones won the Pulitzer Prize for The 1619 Project, a major work published in the *New York Times Magazine* on slavery, its legacy, and the racism that continues to permeate every level of American society. The project proposed to change the nation's founding date from 1776, the year in which the Declaration of Independence was drafted, to 1619, the year that saw the first debarkation of human cargo from Africa in the British colony of Virginia. It also used slavery as the key to interpreting all of American history until the present. Barely a month later, George Floyd died at the hands of the Minneapolis police, sparking some of the most intense anti-racist protests in recent history, which even entailed toppling some monuments to the Founding Fathers.

Black Metropolis

The **Schomburg Center for Research in Black Culture** in Harlem—one of four research centers run by the New York Public Library—is a leading cultural institution dedicated to the documentation of Black life in America. Among its treasures is the initial edition of *Poems on Various Subjects, Religious and Moral* (1773), the first book of verse published by an African American poet—in fact, a female one, Phillis Wheatley. At the time she was purchased as a child by the slave-owning Wheatleys, she had no name, so they assigned her that of the boat that had carried her to Boston after she was kidnapped in West Africa. Upon realizing her exceptional literary skills, her masters exempted her from housework. This was, of course, a golden exception in the deeply slave-ridden America of the late eighteenth century.

↑ The African Burial Ground National Monument honors the more than 15,000 Africans buried in the area between the late 17th and late 18th centuries.

The first African slaves in New Amsterdam arrived in chains in 1625, and were used by the Dutch for agricultural labor and to erect fortifications and stone houses. The English, if anything, were even more cruel: indeed, after a slave market for the sale of men, women, and children opened in New York in 1711, the city became one of the main centers of the slave trade in North America.

By the mid-eighteenth century, Africans amounted to over twenty percent of the colonies' population. In the mid-twentieth century, the epic migration of Europeans to New York was matched by one from the South. Although slavery was formally abolished in the United States only in 1865, New York, like other Northern states, outlawed it prior to the Civil War—more precisely, in 1827. Upon achieving freedom and U.S. citizenship, Blacks nonetheless faced racial segregation and the terror campaigns of the Ku Klux Klan.

For over a century, the heart of New York's African American culture has resided in Harlem, a neighborhood that has retained its toponymic ties with Holland. The key year was 1905, when, following speculation, the real estate value of this large, well-to-do white neighborhood in the northern half of Manhattan plunged, allowing African Americans to purchase their homes. The population shift was quite rapid, so much so that in the 1920s only five out of every hundred inhabitants were white. Thus, before fleeing the South and arriving in Harlem, the young African American King Solomon Gillis, the protagonist in Rudolph Fisher's story "The City of Refuge" (1925), had never seen so many Black people together. He had "no doubt of his whereabouts. This was Negro Harlem . . . [where] black was white [and] you had rights that could not be denied you; you had privileges, protected by law." Overwhelmed, he exclaimed "Done died an' woke up in Heaven."

Scholars have coined the expression "Harlem Renaissance" for this era. Although it is most often associated with jazz, which was closely linked to Prohibition, speakeasies, and venues such as the Cotton Club and its performers of color such as Duke Ellington and Louis Armstrong, Joséphine Baker and Billie Holiday—it marked a blossoming in all the arts. Poetry, fiction, dance, fashion, and theater came to define African American identity and its growing political activism while transforming "social disillusionment into racial pride" (says Alain LeRoy Locke, the informal "Dean" of the movement). The subsequent Wall Street crash and Great Depression seemed like the death knell for this complex movement of Black renewal and self-awareness. It did, however, sow seeds that would flourish in the 1950s and 1960s during the Civil Rights Movement.

The latest census shows a sharp decline in New York City's Black population—a drop of around nine percent over the past twenty years. The prevalence of Blacks in Harlem has been diminishing for at least a decade, a trend similar to that seen in Brooklyn. Driven out by the housing crisis, the rising cost of life, and gentrification, African Americans are moving to other cities, mostly in the South. With its restored brownstones and street art, Harlem, once an area avoided by whites, has been increasingly embraced by the city for its real estate and cultural contrasts. If the trend continues, we will probably see another Black migration, but in the opposite direction.

"A life of blood and tears"

On the night of January 23, 2020, the **Museum of Chinese in America** in Lower Manhattan was nearly consumed by flames. Although tens of thousands of objects in the collection were not harmed by the fire, the water used to put it out caused extensive—but, fortunately, largely reversible—damage. The tragedy, in turn, revealed the value of a unique

← African drummer before a townhouse in Harlem.

↑ The Museum of Chinese in America

collection to Americans and so attracted public and private investments. The headquarters have now been restored and, in the coming years, the collection will see a new home designed by the architect and sculptor Maya Lin.

A restaurant menu, an iron, or embroidered slippers can reveal worlds. Frustrated by the difficulty of finding documents that would help them put together a history of Chinese emigration to America, John Kuo Wei Tchen and Charles Lai, who founded the museum in the late seventies, realized that all they needed could be found in the garbage on the sidewalks, discarded after someone's death or the closing of a shop. Photographs, letters, documents, and objects of all kinds, scraps of lives, snippets of stories about anonymous individuals come together in a grand

→ The annual Lunar New Year parade in Chinatown

communal epic that encompasses hope, exclusion, stereotypes, and tales of racism and discrimination. The great Chinese migration was an epochal phenomenon that began in the mid-nineteenth century, at a time when the rampant demographic growth of the Qing empire dovetailed perfectly with labor demands in the United States. Indeed, the Chinese contributed to the California gold rush and the construction of the Transcontinental Railroad, the first to connect the two coasts. These jobs, to which they dedicated themselves with proverbial pragmatism, were inhumane and insecure. Everything changed in 1882, when the **Chinese Ex-**

To read

- Ralph Ellison, ***Invisible Man*** (1952)
- Toni Morrison, ***Jazz*** (1993)
- Maurizio Molinari, ***The Jews of New York*** (2007)
- Claude McKay, ***Home to Harlem*** (1928)
- Zora Neale Hurston, ***Barracoon: Story of the Last "Black Cargo"*** (2019)
- Deborah Feldman, ***Unorthodox*** (2019)
- Ed Shew, ***Chinese Brothers, American Sons*** (2020)
- James Baldwin, ***The Fire Next Time*** (1963)
- Isaac Bashevis Singer, ***Shadows on the Hudson*** (2021)
- Goldie Goldbloom, ***Madre*** (2023)

clusion Act (repealed only in 1943) blocked entry to further migration and denied Chinese residents in the U.S. the right to citizenship. The "yellow peril" was nothing but a violent hate-filled reaction to the innate resourcefulness of these people, combined with the realization that most of the work for which they had crossed the Pacific was now done. From here it was a short step to the creation of the many Chinatowns in America, in which the Chinese monopolized laundromats, opened diners, and lived in relative isolation.

Lower Manhattan's Chinatown has now subsumed Little Italy, and though traces of its old atmosphere linger, the area is quickly being gentrified. While the African American population is declining, however, that of Asians is rapidly growing: one in seven inhabitants in New York City is Chinese. The more recent immigrants are often more culturally and professionally diverse than their predecessors, and are establishing new Chinatowns in New York, with different accents and businesses. To see these, ride out to **Sunset Park** in Brooklyn, or, better yet, to **Flushing** in Queens—two of the eight current Chinatowns scattered around the city.

Goldene Medine

With around 1.6 million Jews, New York is the world's largest Jewish city, and their numbers, especially those of the Orthodox, are growing. Nearly a quarter of **Brooklyn**'s population is Jewish, of which around two hundred thousand are Hasidic, a fairly closed-off group that include the Satmar, who have recently come under scrutiny on account of their educational system, which was aptly represented in the TV series *Unorthodox*. From Orthodox Russian Jews to those who speak solely Yiddish, from Syrian-Lebanese to Black Jews, from conservative to reformed and queer-friendly communities, the entire panoply of Judaism is represented in the city.

▲ Boys in Borough Park, Brooklyn

The first twenty-three Jewish refugees arrived in New Amsterdam in 1654 to escape the Portuguese who had replaced the more tolerant Dutch in Recife, Brazil. Some initial resistance eventually gave way to the "great exception in the Jewish people's history"—as historian Jonathan Sarna put it, namely, coexistence of Jews and Gentiles on American soil, where anti-Semitism did not lead to open persecution.

Jewish New York came into being at the beginning of the 20th century, when a million Jews fled Lithuania, Russia, and Poland due to famines and the anti-Semitic pogroms following the assassination of Tsar Alexander II. Settling initially in the dilapidated and unhealthy tenements on the Lower East Side, those who could afford it eventually moved to

School bus passing through Borough Park, Brooklyn

To watch

- Gordon Parks, ***Shaft*** (1971)
- Joan Micklin Silver, ***Hester Street*** (1975)
- Francis Ford Coppola, ***Cotton Club*** (1984)
- Michael Cimino, ***Year of the Dragon*** (1985)
- Eddie Murphy, ***Harlem Nights*** (1989)
- Spike Lee, ***Malcolm X*** (1992)
- Lee Daniels, ***Precious*** (2009)
- William McGregor, ***One of Us*** (2016), TV miniseries
- Evan Jackson Leong, ***Snakehead*** (2021)
- James Gray, ***Armageddon Time*** (2022)

Brooklyn over the Williamsburg Bridge that joined the two banks of the East River. Here, in Williamsburg, Borough Park, Crown Heights, and Flatbush, they founded synagogues, congregations, and yeshivahs (religious schools) as well as myriad shops. To this day, the concentration of Jewish businesses in this area is astonishing.

On September 8, 1945, Bess Myerson was selected Miss America. Although World War II had come to an end only several days prior with the surrender of Japan, the horrors of Auschwitz had already come to light earlier that year. Myerson did not experience the anti-Semitism that had led to the massacre of entire communities in the Old World, but when she refused to change her Jewish surname before the competition, some of its sponsors withdrew and several performers cancelled their appearances. This, of course, was a minor issue compared to the worrisome recent increase in the number of anti-Semitic and anti-Zionist episodes of intolerance and violence throughout the country that have been recorded by civil rights groups and movements. In late 2018, a man shot and killed eleven people at a Pittsburgh synagogue. Though 2022 was a record year for attacks, many of which took place in Brooklyn, New York's ties to Israel remain solid. Each year, on the day of the State of Israel's founding, thousands of flags with the Star of David paired with the Stars and Stripes adorn the street lamps of Fifth Avenue, while the Empire State Building is lit up in white and blue, the colors of the flag of Israel, even if today the United States seems somewhat less of a less safe haven or *"Goldene Medine"*—the Ashkenazi term for "Golden Land"—for Jews.

▸ Two children walking to the synagogue in Williamsburg, Brooklyn

William Dello Russo

An historian of art, he also writes, edits, and does iconographical research for the principal Italian publishing houses specializing in art and tourism.

Captions of the photographic insert

pages 70-71 Ice skating in Central Park

page 72 Stock Exchange Building on Wall Street

page 73 Grand Central Terminal

page 74 Brooklyn Bridge from Dumbo

page 75 Rooftop water towers

page 76 Chrysler Building

page 77 Manhattanhenge in Midtown around the time of the summer solstice

page 78 Mermaid Parade in Coney Island

page 79 Luna Park in Coney Island

page 80-81 Central Park and Billionaires' Row

page 82 Subway in Queens

page 83 Queensboro Bridge

page 84 Waiting for the subway at Penn Station

page 85 Steam vents in Manhattan

page 86 A fire escape

page 87 Lower Manhattan from an airplane window

pages 88-89 The Lunar New Year parade in Chinatown

Photo Credits

page 2 NYC Russ/Shutterstock

page 5 Francois Roux/Shutterstock

page 8 Frederick Millett/Shutterstock

page 12 Bettmann/Bettmann/Getty Images

page 13 Bettmann/Bettmann/Getty Images

page 14 George Rinhart/Corbis Historical /Getty Images

page 16 Sean Pavone/Shutterstock

page 17 gary718/Shutterstock

page 18 C. Taylor Crothers/ Getty Images Entertainment/Getty Images

page 21 David Pereiras/Shutterstock

page 25 THEPALMER/E+/Getty Images

page 26 Rodolpho de Souza/Shutterstock

page 27 Angelo Hornak/Corbis Historical /Getty Images

page 29 C. Taylor Crothers/Getty Images News /Getty Images

page 30 Ritu Manoj Jethani/Shutterstock

page 33 China News Service/China News Service/ Getty Images

page 34 The Metropolitan Museum of Art, New York, The Cloisters Collection, 1935 (Open Access)

page 37 David Grossman/Alamy Foto Stock

page 39 INTERFOTO/Alamy Foto Stock

page 40 Taiga/Shutterstock

page 43 Robert Alexander/Archive Photos /Getty Images

page 45 rarrarorro/Shutterstock

ppage 48-49 Cindy Ord/Getty Images Entertainment/Getty Images

page 50 C. Taylor Crothers/Getty Images Entertainment/Getty Images

page 54 dibrova/Shutterstock

page 56 Pit Stock/Shutterstock

page 57 Gabriel Murad/Shutterstock

page 58 Randy Duchaine / Alamy Foto Stock

page 59 Gary Hershorn/Corbis News /Getty Images

page 60 Anadolu Agency/Anadolu Agency /Getty Images

page 63 Jim McIsaac/Getty Images Sport /Getty Images

ù page 64 Al Bello/Getty Images Sport /Getty Images
page 66 Jim McIsaac/Getty Images Sport /Getty Images
page 69 Debby Wong/Shutterstock
ppage 70-71 Stuart Monk/Shutterstock
page 72 ventdusud/Shutterstock
page 73 Resul Muslu/Shutterstock
page 74 Jerome LABOUYRIE/Shutterstock
page 75 lazyllama/Shutterstock
page 76 Hoberman Collection/Universal Images Group/Getty Images
page 77 Ryan DeBerardinis/Shutterstock
page 78 DON EMMERT/AFP/Getty Images
page 79 quietbits/Shutterstock
ppage 80-81 C. Taylor Crothers/Getty Images Entertainment/Getty Images
page 82 Joseph Giardino/Shutterstock
page 83 Edi Chen/Shutterstock
page 84 littlenySTOCK/Shutterstock
page 85 Iryna Horbachova/Shutterstock
page 86 photoiva/Shutterstock
page 87 HASAN AKBAS/Shutterstock
ppage 88-89 ANDREA RENAULT/AFP /Getty Images
page 90 Spencer Platt/Getty Images News /Getty Images
page 93 Kent Nishimura/Los Angeles Times /Getty Images
page 94 Spencer Platt/Getty Images News /Getty Images
page 95 MatthieuCattin/Shutterstock
ppage 96-97 Carl Tomich/Shutterstock
page 98 Chris Hondros/Getty Images News /Getty Images
page 102 Andia/Universal Images Group /Getty Images
page 105 Madelyn Mills/Shutterstock
page 108 nito/Shutterstock
page 110 Eileen_10/Shutterstock
page 111 Henry Veloso/Shutterstock
page 112 Patti McConville/Alamy Foto Stock
page 115 STAN HONDA/AFP/Getty Images
page 117 Rainer Grosskopf/ Stockbyte Unreleased/ Getty Images
page 118 Stacy Walsh Rosenstock/ Alamy Foto Stock
page 119 Christian Mueller/Shutterstock
page 120 DON EMMERT/AFP/Getty Images
page 123 Noam Galai/ Getty Images Entertainment/Getty Images
page 124 GagliardiPhotography/Shutterstock
page 128 littlenySTOCK/Shutterstock
page 129 DOMINICK REUTER/AFP /Getty Images
page 130 RuslanKphoto/Shutterstock
page 131 Yaaaashverma/Shutterstock
page 132 Richard Levine/Alamy Foto Stock
page 134 Brian Hamill/Premium Archive /Getty Images
page 137 Jason Sponseller/Shutterstock
page 139 sdf_qwe/Shutterstock
page 142 Drew Angerer/Getty Images News /Getty Images
page 144 DON EMMERT/AFP/Getty Images
page 145 UCG/ Universal Images Group /Getty Images
page 146 STAN HONDA/AFP/Getty Images
page 149 Roy Rochlin/ Getty Images Entertainment/Getty Images
page 150 Here Now/Shutterstock
page 152 Michael M. Santiago /Getty Images News/Getty Images
page 153 ANDREA RENAULT/AFP/Getty Images
page 155 VIEW press/Corbis News/Getty Images
page 156 Spencer Platt/Getty Images News /Getty Images
page 157 Creative Supreme NYC/Shutterstock

Cover ??

Acknowledgments

Writing a book on New York is not easy. This one joins the thousands of monographs devoted to the city that never sleeps, adding yet another piece to the unique adventure that is New York. Special thanks go to Flavio Caprera and Tommaso Guaita, who have revealed to me the city's musical secrets and sports crazes.

Concept and Editorial Project
Balthazar Pagani / BesideBooks

Graphic Design and Layout
Bebung

Photo Research
William Dello Russo

Piazzale Luigi Cadorna, 6
20123 Milan, Italy
www.whitestar.it

Translation: Irina Oryshkevich
Editing: Phillip Gaskill

ISBN 978-88-544-2042-7
1 2 3 4 5 6 28 27 26 25 24

Printed in China

MIX
Paper from responsible sources
FSC® C178000